A GUARDED SECRET

Tsar Nicholas II, Tsarina Alexandra and Tsarevich Alexei's Hemophilia

Julia P Gelardi

AUTHOR'S NOTE

This book is part of a series, "**ROYAL CAVALCADE**," designed to give the reader a glimpse into the world of Europe's royal families and the impact their lives had on history. I've chosen to show this by focusing on a particular aspect in the fascinating, moving, and often complicated personal and political lives of royalty.

Each book is for the general reader in that those with no prior knowledge of each topic can easily read the book without feeling the need to have had prior exposure to the topic. Specialist readers - those who have extensive knowledge of the subject - can also benefit from the book because the emphasis on a particular topic can lend new or extensive light on existing knowledge.

Thank you for purchasing this book, and if have enjoyed reading this book from my series, "**ROYAL CAVALCADE**," I'd be most grateful if you could post on Amazon a brief review and read as well, other books from the series. Thanks again, and don't forget to visit my website at juliapgelardi.com.

Calendar/Dates Used: Russia used the Julian calendar (Old Style, O.S.) until January 1918 when the Bolsheviks adopted the Gregorian calendar, and consequently until this change occurred the Russian calendar tended to be behind by 12 days in relation to the Western calendar. The dates used throughout this book are in the Old Style.

Russian Names: Russian names consist of the first name, the middle or patronymic, and the last. The patronymic is derived from the father's first name. For males, the patronymic ends in "ovich" or "evich." Hence, "Nicholas Alexandrovich" is Nicholas, son of Alexander. "Alexei Nikolaevich" is Alexei, son of Nicholas.

For females, the patronymic ends in "ovna" or "evna." Hence, "Olga Alexandrovna" is Olga, daughter of Alexander. "Tatiana Nikolaevna" is Tatiana, daughter of Nicholas.

Russian Titles: The rulers of Russia since Peter the Great (r. 1682-1725) are designated as "Emperor." However, "Tsar," or "Czar" has been used as well. The consorts of rulers have been referred to as "Tsaritsa" or "Tsarina." The male heir of the emperor was the "Tsesarevich," but the title "Tsarevich" has also been used. Daughters were "Grand Duchesses" and younger sons, "Grand Dukes." In this book, the titles "Tsar" and "Emperor" as well as "Tsarina" and "Empress" are used interchangeably. "Tsarevich" is used instead of "Tsesarevich."

S

∞ Queen Victoria = Prince Albert of Saxe-Coburg-Gotha

∞ Princess Alice = Louis IV of Hesse

Tsar Alexander III = Dagmar of Denmark

Tsar Nicholas II (1868-1918) = ∞ Tsarina Alexandra Feodorovna (1872-1918)

Olga (1895-1918) Tatiana (1897-1918) Marie (1899-1918) Anastasia (1901-18) Alexei (1904-18)

Table of Contents

Author's Note   i

Simplified Genealogical Table   iv

Chapter 1   "A Great and Unforgettable Day" (1904)   1

Chapter 2   A Stunning Relevation (1904-1905)   14

Chapter 3   "Their Heaviest Cross (1906-1911)"   29

Chapter 4   Rasputin (1906-1912)   42

Illustrations   54

Chapter 5   Spala (1912) and Tercentenary

        Celebrations (1913)   59

Chapter 6   The War Years (1914-1917)   71

Chapter 7   Revolution (1917)   103

Chapter 8   Captivity (1917-1918)   122

Epilogue   149

Did you enjoy this book?   151

Endnotes   152

Bibliography   181

Further Reading   186

About the Author   188

Chapter 1. "A Great and Unforgettable Day" (1904)

Russia in the summer of 1904 was not a tranquil place. The country was enveloped in a state of anxiety. Fortune had not shone brightly on the vast empire that stretched from the Baltic Sea in the west to the Pacific Ocean in the east. Engulfed in an increasingly bitter war in the Far East against Japan, Russia was also wracked by domestic instability. In June, Nikolai Brobikov, Russia's Governor-General in Finland, was assassinated. In the end of July, the Russian Minister of the Interior, Vyacheslav Plehve, was also killed when an assassin threw a bomb at Plehve's carriage. Agitation against tsarist autocratic rule was increasing in fervor; and the Tsar who was in the crosshairs of these enemies of autocracy was Nicholas II.

Ten years before, Tsar Nicholas II had ascended the throne. Within weeks of his accession, the twenty-six-year-old Nicholas II wed in the chapel of the Winter Palace in St. Petersburg,

Alexandra, the former Princess Alix of Hesse and by Rhine. The twenty-two-year-old Tsarina Alexandra was a favorite granddaughter of Queen Victoria, who had at first opposed the match, but eventually accepted it. The marriage of Nicholas and Alexandra had been a genuine love match and the couple was devoted to each other. Before the end of 1895, the couple eagerly awaited the birth of their first child, hoping that a son and heir would be born.

Ever since the Emperor Paul I had decreed in 1797 that the succession to the throne of the Russian Empire could only be through the male line, none of the wives of the Russian emperors since then had failed in giving the country the coveted male heir. It thus came as no surprise that Tsarina Alexandra felt the burden of having to provide her husband with a son as soon as possible.

When Alexandra had given birth to their first child, Grand Duchess Olga Nikolaevna, in November 1895, the Tsarina, tears stinging her eyes, had reportedly apologized to the Tsar for the arrival of a daughter. Undeterred, Nicholas II replied that, "I am extremely pleased to have a little girl. This child is ours, and ours alone. If a son had been born, it would not have been so. He would have belonged to Russia."

When her second child, Grand Duchess Tatiana Nikolaevna, was born in 1897, the disappointment felt by Tsarina Alexandra was even stronger than when Olga had been born. "My God, it is again a daughter," Alexandra was reported to have said soon after giving birth for the second time; and then bursting into hot tears, she sobbed, "what will the nation say, what will the nation say?"

The Tsarina had once admitted that her unpopularity was connected to the fact that she had failed to provide her husband with a son, prompting her to admit: "What good does it do me to be loved by my husband when all the world is against me? It is the nation's love I would wish to win, and how can I hope to do so, so long as I have not given an heir to Russia!"

In 1899 Tsarina Alexandra gave birth again; and like her two previous births, this child had turned out to be another girl, the Grand Duchess Marie Nikolaevna. Alexandra had failed again. There was still no male heir.

As the years passed with no son to give
Russia, Tsarina Alexandra became increasingly
desperate. She had prayed fervently for years to
present the nation with an heir, and with each
passing year where no son arrived, Alexandra
became prey to several so-called people of faith
who claimed to be able to help her. One such
individual, a Frenchman by the name of Philippe
Nazier-Vachot, had been introduced to her by
Grand Duchess Militza, the daughter of King
Nicholas I of Montenegro. Militza, along with her
sister, Anastasia, had married into the Romanov
family and wielded some influence with the
Tsarina. They found in Nazier-Vachot a supposed
'faith healer' who was worthy of being presented to
the imperial couple. The Tsarina met him in 1901
and ignored warnings that he was not to be trusted.
Philippe was duly welcomed at court; and
Alexandra believed that he had an ability to
determine an unborn baby's sex. But Philippe's
fortune faded when the Tsarina gave birth to yet
another girl, Grand Duchess Anastasia Nikolaevna,
in 1901. When she was born, the Tsar, in his
disappointment, had to take a long walk in the park

to compose himself before he faced his wife and newborn daughter.

Philippe was eventually sent away after declaring that the Tsarina was pregnant in 1903 even though she was not. But before he left, Philippe told the Tsarina of what was in store for her in the future: "You will someday have another friend like me who will speak to you of God."

Despite the Philippe Nazier-Vachot episode, Tsarina Alexandra continued to look for help, and did not ignore Grand Duchess Militza when she suggested that the empress seek the intercession of a holy man, Seraphim of Sarov, who had died in 1833. Tsarina Alexandra insisted amidst some opposition, that Seraphim be canonized as a saint. He was duly declared a saint. Nicholas and Alexandra and several members of the imperial family and thousands of fellow pilgrims had journeyed to Sarov where Seraphim's remains were interred in the cathedral. The Tsarina bathed in the Sarov River, reputed to have healing powers attributed to Seraphim, and prayed at the saint's shrine, all in the hopes of giving birth to a son. Within months she was pregnant.

As was customary during the summer months, Nicholas and Alexandra decamped in 1904 to Peterhof, the extensive imperial estate located some twenty-four miles west of the Russian capital, St. Petersburg. Home for them at Peterhof was the Lower Dacha, a striking yellow and red brick villa, built in the 1880s for the future Nicholas II in the Italianate style. Its proximity to the Gulf of Finland meant that the imperial family could enjoy the cool gulf breezes and picturesque views of the water. On July 30, 1904, however, the Tsar's attention was focused not on the views from his villa, but on the impending birth of his fifth child.

The day had been uncomfortably hot, and Nicholas and Alexandra had just sat down to lunch. Soon after finishing her soup, Alexandra excused herself and went to her room. Anxiety and excitement swept the villa. The Tsarina was in labor. Alexandra, who always had trouble with her pregnancies and birth, had been blessed at this latest confinement with a labor and birth that passed relatively quickly. After a hushed silence descended on the room where Alexandra lay, a baby's loud cry pierced the air. Dr. Ott, the Tsarina's physician, turned to a nervous and pale Tsar, anxious about his wife and newborn child. Dr. Ott's words stunned Nicholas II: "I congratulate Your Majesty on the birth of a Czarevitsch."

So shocked was the Tsar at the happy news, that he stood dazed, unable to utter any words. The Tsarina, who had been under the effects of chloroform, soon opened her eyes and sought her husband's face. When Alexandra saw Nicholas' joy, she dared to express what she had prayed so hard for: "Oh, it cannot be true; it cannot be true. Is it really a boy?"

By way of an answer, the Tsar fell on his knees and sobbed tears of joy by his wife's side. To the Tsarina, her newborn baby boy was the answer to her many prayers, the culmination of her marriage to Nicholas II, and the hope of the Russian people.

The sheer joy and relief at being the father at last of a son and heir are encapsulated in the words Nicholas II wrote in his diary: "A great and unforgettable day for us, during which we were clearly visited by the grace of God." Nicholas also wrote: "There are no words to thank God enough for sending us this comfort in a time of sore trials!" Those "sore trials" referred to by the Tsar was the

Russo-Japanese War raging in Manchuria, inflicting humiliating and painful losses for the Russians, casting a heavy pall upon the nation. Alexei's birth was thus a ray of joyful news amidst a year that was full of troubles for Russia. The boy's birth was of such great magnitude and importance that one contemporary reported that "it absorbed for some time the whole attention of the public and diverted it from all that was taking place in the Far East."

When the birth of an heir to the throne was announced, the "wildest rejoicings" erupted "all over the Empire." Cities, towns, and villages all over Russia broke out in celebration. In the capital, the Tsar's subjects learned of the happy event when the large cannons of the Fortress of Saints Peter and Paul boomed. One hundred-one shots meant that the baby born was a girl. When the cannons thundered the one hundred second shot, excitement rose until the full three hundred-and-one shots for a boy were given. Cathedrals and church bells pealed all over the city in joyous celebration. Nicholas II's sister, Grand Duchess Olga Alexandrovna, recalled, "how happy the people looked when the news was announced." Grand Duke Nicholas, a cousin of the Tsar's, recorded in his diary that, "God has sent their Majesties a son. What a joy! Russia has waited 10 years for an Heir, and now it has happened."

When that longed-for son had finally been born, Nicholas and Alexandra named him Alexei in honor of Nicholas II's favorite ancestor, Tsar Alexei, who reigned in the seventeenth century. The name also connoted 'bringer of peace.' As it turned out, the Tsarevich Alexei was the first heir born to a ruling emperor since the seventeenth century.

The arrival of a new boy in the family did not cause any jealousy from the four daughters of the Tsar and Tsarina. Margaretta Eager, the Irish nurse of the four Grand Duchesses, noted how "the little sisters were delighted with the new brother, and made many quaint and critical remarks about him."

Alexei's baptism took place in the golden cupolaed chapel of the Grand Palace at Peterhof, a mere twelve days after his birth. The baptism was a splendid and formal occasion that saw the imperial court's full participation. The men appeared in full dress uniforms and the women in beautiful Russian court dress. The little Grand Duchesses looked delightful in their short court dresses of blue satin and silver trimming along with matching pearl-embroidered *kokoshniks* on their heads. The Tsarevich rode to the ceremony in a gilt coach drawn by eight horses. Numerous regimental soldiers lined the route. The baby's godparents included the Dowager Empress Marie Feodorovna, his paternal grandmother; his great-uncle, Grand Duke Alexei Alexandrovich; his sister, Grand Duchess Olga Nikolaevna; King Christian IX of Denmark; England's King Edward VII, along with Kaiser Wilhelm II of Germany; and for honorary godfathers, the soldiers fighting for Russia in far-off Manchuria, were chosen. As tradition dictated, the baby Tsarevich was carried by the elderly Mistress of the Robes, Princess Maria Golitzyna. She had rubber soles placed on her shoes so as to avoid slipping while carrying the precious heir who lay on a pillow made of cloth-of-gold. A gold-colored band was slung over the Princess's shoulder as well, another precaution to prevent the heir from being dropped. The imperial family's confessor and the priest who had assisted the Tsarina with her conversion to Orthodoxy, Father Yanishev, dipped the baby in the baptismal font.

Alexei made his presence known, crying lustily for all to hear.

Margaretta Eagar, who was present, recalled of the Tsarevich Alexei: "In the middle of the baptismal ceremony, when he was being anointed for the first time, he raised his hand and extended his fingers as though pronouncing a blessing. Of course, everyone said that it was a very good omen, and that he would prove to be a father to his people." Eagar added, "God grant it, but not for many years to come."

For one so young, the list of titles and honors the baby received was impressive: His Imperial Highness, Sovereign Heir and Tsesarevich, Grand Duke Alexei Nikolaevich of Russia, Ataman of All Cossacks, Knight of the Order of St. Andrew, Head of the Siberian Infantry, of the Horse Battalion Infantry, and Head of the Cadet Corps. Nor was Alexei's pedigree any less impressive. Through his father, he descended from Emperors of Russia. His paternal great-grandfather was King Christian IX of Denmark. Through his mother, Alexei was a great-grandson of Britain's venerable Queen Victoria.

Tsar Nicholas understandably felt happy, relieved and proud to have fathered a son. But the Tsarina was even more overjoyed by the event. Soon after Tsarevich Alexei was born, his mother had referred to him to his father as "a real Sunbeam." Alexandra told Nicholas, "and now you have him to work for and to bring up to your ideas, so as that he can help you…" The Tsarina also wrote to her husband, "Oh God is indeed good having sent in this sunbeam now, when we all need it so much, may He give us the force to bring Baby up well – and to be a real help and comrade to you when he is a big."

At home, the baby Alexei had joined a family consisting of his parents, Tsar Nicholas II who was thirty-five-years old; Tsarina Alexandra, thirty-two, and four sisters: Olga, nine; Tatiana, seven; Marie, five; and Anastasia, three. From the day of his birth, Alexei was showered with love and affection from his close-knit family. The wonder and enchantment with which the little Tsarevich's sisters held their little brother from his early days were echoed by others who had the good fortune of making His Imperial Highness's acquaintance as a baby. A senior courtier who met the baby Tsarevich described Alexei as a "chubby, rosy – a wonderful boy!"

The baby who was born weighing over ten pounds appeared healthy and full of life. His paternal aunt, the Grand Duchess Xenia, saw Alexei in his bath two weeks after his birth, and noted, "he's an amazingly hefty baby, with a chest like a barrel and generally has the air of a warrior knight." Margaretta Eagar recorded of the new heir that "he is a very beautiful boy."

The early first weeks of Alexei's life were full of hope and happiness. The family was complete. The dynasty's succession was secured. All of Tsarina Alexandra's prayers had been answered. Her bouncing blue-eyed baby boy with "the air of a warrior knight" was all she could hope for.

But dark clouds were set to appear on the horizon. An ominous sign was soon to make its mark, sending Nicholas and Alexandra's world crashing.

Chapter 2.   A Stunning Revelation (1904 – 1905)

Having at last given birth to the longed-for male heir, Tsarina Alexandra had gained more confidence and her previous unpopularity waned. Her delicate health, previous pregnancies, plus suspicion of St. Petersburg high society, had all contributed to Alexandra's need and desire to keep away from the capital. But with the arrival of Alexei, the Tsarina began to socialize. Large scale entertainments may have been out of the question while the Russo-Japanese War raged, but Alexandra began to host small parties for some members of society. Had good news out of the Far East for the Russian armed forces been forthcoming, the Tsarina would have likely continued to increase her entertainments. But no such good news came. Instead, by the end of 1904, Port Arthur, the Russian naval base in Manchuria, fell. And closer to home, another harrowing incident hit the imperial couple – an incident that would lead to tragedy for Russia.

On the 8th of September 1904, Tsar Nicholas recorded in his diary: "Alix and I were very worried because little Alexei started bleeding from the navel, and it continued on and off until the evening!" In fact, the Tsarevich bled on and off for several days. The bleeding episode confirmed the terrible news that baby Alexei was a hemophiliac.

The news was devastating. There had already been hints that Alexei might be a hemophiliac. When the umbilical cord had been cut at birth, the baby bled. It took the doctors two days to control it. One of the Tsar's relatives, Grand Duke Peter, and his wife, Grand Duchess Militza, had visited Nicholas and Alexandra on the day of Alexei's birth to offer their good wishes. Upon departing, the Tsar admitted to the Grand Duke that there were concerns about the Tsarevich bleeding. Militza, when she learned of this, later spoke to the Tsar by telephone, and "with the calmest of voices," begged him to ask the doctors if there were sings of hemophilia. The telephone call ended with Nicholas II "quietly repeating the word that had staggered him: haemophlia."

Nicholas and Alexandra's precious only son was destined to have a life of suffering, and most likely to live a short life. The chubby, healthy looking baby with the fair curls turned out to be sickly. Hemophilia was incurable and condemned male sufferers to bleed easily because of an inability of their blood to clot. The slightest cut and lightest bump could trigger painful attacks of internal and external bleeding that could prove fatal. A hemophiliac could hemorrhage for hours and days on end – bleeding episodes that could result in rock-hard hematomas. There was also the possibility that a hemophiliac could be crippled should the joints bleed, an episode that could bring excruciating pain. And once the blood entered a joint, it could wreak havoc, permanently damaging the bone and everything around it. The fact that hemophilia was unpredictable made it impossible to prevent attacks. Weeks and months could go by without a minor episode, and then, all-of-a-sudden, an attack would ensue, and the difficult task of helping the victim began. It was a painful vigil that required a combination of prayer and giving the hemophiliac the best possible care available to science at the time. Such, then, became the pattern of life for Nicholas and Alexandra, and Alexei.

Upon learning of that their son was a hemophiliac, the Tsar and Tsarina were under no illusions about the disease. The imperial couple was all too aware of hemophilia's affects on its victims. The Tsarina had inherited the fatal gene from her maternal grandmother, England's Queen Victoria. Alexandra's own mother passed the gene to her. The Tsarina's young brother, Prince Friedrich of Hesse, was a hemophiliac and died at the age of three. Her uncle, Prince Leopold, a son of Queen Victoria, was also afflicted with the disease and died at the age of thirty. Hemophilia also afflicted two of the three sons of the Tsarina's sister, Princess Irene. These nephews were born in 1899 and 1900; and the youngest, Prince Heinrich, died at the age of four not long before Alexei's birth.

The hemophilia gene also made an impact on the royal family of Spain where Tsarina Alexandra's cousin, Queen Victoria Eugenie, passed on the gene to two of her sons, including the eldest son and heir, the Prince of the Asturias. The fact that the Queen of Spain brought the deadly gene into the Spanish royal family had tragic consequences, for it created a rift in the marriage of Queen Victoria Eugenie and King Alfonso XIII. The same, however, could not be said when it came the Tsar Nicholas II and Tsarina Alexandra. Nicholas never faltered in his love for his wife despite the fact that she had passed the deadly hemophilia gene on to their only son.

The fact that Tsarevich Alexei inherited the deadly gene from his mother affected Tsarina Alexandra deeply. Already a serious character and shy with society, Alexandra turned even more inward, preferring the company of her family and the few close courtiers she felt she could count on. One of the Tsar's relatives wrote that when Alexandra realized that Alexei suffered from hemophilia, "from that moment, troubled and apprehensive, the Empress's character underwent a change, and her health, physical as well as moral, altered."

The Tsar's brother-in-law, Grand Duke Alexander, known as 'Sandro,' recalled how Nicholas II, upon being stunned by the news of his son's hemophilia, had aged ten years overnight. "He could not bear," wrote Sandro, "that his only son, his lovable Alexis, stood condemned by medical science either to die at an early age or lead the existence of an invalid."

Tsarina Alexandra feared that should the nation learn the extent of the heir's malady, it would bode ill for the dynasty. Both Nicholas and Alexandra firmly believed that autocracy, where power is held and exercised by the Emperor, was best suited to Russia, where it had been the form of government for centuries. At Nicholas II's coronation in 1896, when he had been crowned Autocrat and Emperor of All the Russias, Nicholas had also sworn to preserve autocracy – an oath he took seriously. Consequently, Nicholas and Alexandra perceived that any diminution of autocracy went against the Tsar's solemn oath and was bound to be detrimental to Russia. An invalid in the form of Russia's next monarch could embolden opponents of Nicholas and Alexandra to promote other family members as more suitable heirs, such as the Tsar's younger brother, Grand Duke Michael. If this were allowed to happen, disunity could ensue, leading to unforeseen troubles. Then there was the delicate issue of the Tsarina's unpopularity. What little popularity the Tsarina may have gained at finally giving birth to a son was likely to be lost if everyone knew just how precarious the health of Alexei was, and that Alexandra was the cause of it. Moreover, the Tsarina was already inclined to believe that her family life should be kept private. All this, then, combined to compel the imperial couple to keep the Tsarevich's illness a closely guarded secret.

In no time, a cocoon of protection enveloped the Tsarevich Alexei. Already living in the Alexander Palace at Tsarskoe Selo in self-imposed exile from St. Petersburg, the Empress insisted that they continue to reside there where it was far easier to keep Alexei's condition to themselves. Isolating themselves at Tsarskoe Selo had been effective. Not many knew of the heir's malady outside of a close circle of family and loyal retainers. Abroad, the coverage of the baby Alexei at this point gave no clue of the child's hemophilia. A major British newspaper, upon publishing Alexei's photograph for the first time in the United Kingdom in February 1905, noted how he "has always been a remarkably healthy child." The coverage continued with another photograph of the entire imperial family with the Tsarevich in the center of the tableaux in his mother's arms. The caption noted how, "the Czar is immensely proud of his son, for whom he had waited so long."

After surviving his initial serious bout of bleeding at the age of six weeks, Tsarevich Alexei grew, gained weight, and thrived as if he had been a normal baby. Tsar Nicholas could not resist showing off the months-old heir to A.A. Mossolov, Head of the Court Chancellery. The imperial family were cruising the Finnish fjords on the yacht, the *Standart*, at the time. The Tsar invited Mossolov to meet the young heir.

"Don't you think he's a beauty?" said Nicholas II.

Mossolov recalled how, "the Tsar went on talking to me of his son's strong constitution."

"His legs," continued the proud father, "are in good proportion with his body. And best of all, what lovely 'bracelets' he has on his wrists and ankles! He's well nourished!"

The Tsarevich continued to flourish and by the time Alexei was a year-and-a-half old, the Tsar boasted to his mother, the Dowager Empress Marie Feodorovna, that "he can walk quite well…"

It came as no surprise that the Tsarina doted on Alexei, her only son. Baroness Sophie

Buxhoeveden, one of the Tsarina's ladies-in-waiting, confirmed this, stating that, "the Empress's favourite child, the one on whom all her thoughts were centred, was her boy."

Tsarina Alexandra and Tsar Nicholas's attempts to keep their son's illness a secret was successful in Alexei's early years. An American publication had made no mention of anything amiss with the Tsarevich's health in a complimentary article on the Tsarina, extolling her "quiet home life." The article ended on an optimistic note, telling its readers that, "disastrous storms have raged outside, but within the sacred circle of her home life the young Czarina has found peace and happiness."

As happy as the Tsarina may have been in the domestic sphere, notwithstanding Alexei's hemophilia, events within Russia gave the Tsar and Tsarina cause for tremendous concern. The year 1905, in particular turned, out to be a harrowing year. When Alexei was a mere six months old an event that came to be known as 'Bloody Sunday' shook the monarchy. On a cold, snowy January Sunday, troops descended on St. Petersburg, with many of them surrounding the Winter Palace in order to protect it. Over 100,000 workers marched toward the palace, headed by an Orthodox priest, Fr. Gapon. The peaceful protestors, many carrying religious banners and icons and portraits of Nicholas II were intent on presenting their petition to the Tsar, asking for better working conditions and universal suffrage. The Tsar, however, was not at the Winter Palace, but at Tsarskoe Selo. Orders were given to keep the massive crowd of workers from arriving at the Winter Palace. Confusion and panic reigned. Soldiers fired. Before the end of the day, over 100 marchers had been killed and 800 injured. Not only were lives destroyed, Bloody Sunday had also rent asunder what goodwill the workers had for the Tsar. What in effect occurred was that "Nicholas II, failing to grasp that a profound shift in public opinion had happened, moved himself and the Romanovs one more step toward political extinction." And the as it turned out, "the first Romanov to pay the price was (the Tsar's uncle) the Grand Duke Serge Alexandrovich."

In February 1905 the Tsar's uncle, the Grand Duke Serge, the unpopular former Governor General of Moscow, was killed in that city when a terrorist threw a bomb at his carriage. Serge's wife, Ella, who was also Tsarina Alexandra's sister, heard the explosion, rushed out onto the scene and picked up fragments of her husband's shattered body and placed them in her palace chapel. The Tsar could not attend his uncle's funeral; it was deemed to dangerous for him to leave Tsarskoe Selo for Moscow. The Grand Duke Konstantin Konstantinovich did attend the funeral and afterwards admitted in his diary his worries about the country's troubles: "These terrible events seem like some kind of dream. In Russia everything is getting worse; if you look back at the autumn, to September and October, you simply can't believe with what quick steps we have advanced to disaster, to unknown misfortunes."

Those disasters and misfortunes continued to mount. Soon after Grand Duke Serge's funeral, the Japanese defeated the Russians in a massive land battle at Mukden, inflicting heavy casualties on the Russians, amounting to nearly 90,000 soldiers. In May, the Japanese again defeated the Russians, this time at the naval Battle of Tsushima that lasted for two days. This major, humiliating defeat saw Russia's Baltic fleet annihilated. Over

4,000 Russian sailors were killed and nearly 6,000 captured. In June, Russian sailors of the Black Sea fleet mutinied on the battleship, *Potemkin*. This nefarious incident became "a powerful icon of revolution," and the Tsar in anger noted that "only the devil knows what is happening to the Black Sea fleet."

Strikes and unrest continued to spread throughout the country. Conceding defeat in the Russo-Japanese War, the Russians signed the Treaty of Portsmouth in August, ending the war. To deal with the growing chaos in his empire, the Tsar had agreed to limited consultative assemblies to look into constitutional reforms. In August, he agreed to the creation of a Duma or legislative assembly, but it was seen as too weak by the revolutionaries because of its small electorate. As the months passed, chaos and near anarchy prevailed in Russia as strikes practically crippled St. Petersburg, Moscow, and other large swathes of the nation. Violent clashes between soldiers and ordinary citizens were widespread. What support the Tsar and Tsarina had among the people fell even more. Revolution threatened to bring the Russian Empire to its knees. In an emotional letter to his mother, the Tsar wrote: "It makes me sick to read the news! Nothing but new strikes in schools and factories, murdered policemen, Cossacks and soldiers, riots, disorders, mutinies."

Nicholas II did not exaggerate his brutal assessment of the state of his empire. For "few countries have ever seen such a general strike as developed in Russia." From bakers to factory workers, stockbrokers and doctors, even the corps de ballet of the famed Mariinksy theater all went on strike. The water supply of St. Petersburg was endangered. It was kept safe only because the authorities took the drastic measure of locking its workers in. There was practically no electricity in St. Petersburg, making the city "as dark as it had been in the Middle Ages." Russia was near collapse.

Sergei Witte, the respected former finance minister, was called in to help the Tsar resolve the rapidly deteriorating situation. Witte noted how, "a feeling of profound dejection reigned at the court." There were few options left, as Nicholas II explained to his mother: either "crush the rebellion by sheer force" which in the end "would mean rivers of blood" or "give to the people their civil rights, freedom of speech and press, also to have all laws confirmed by a State Duma – that, of course, would be a constitution."

With great reluctance, and with a trembling hand, Tsar Nicholas signed the October Manifesto which granted a constitutional government to Russia. With the stroke of a pen, the Tsar had acquiesced to an unheard-of step: the dilution of his power. He was no longer an autocrat. It was difficult for Nicholas to accept this, for he had sworn at his coronation on the sacredness of the powers he had been granted as emperor – powers which were to be passed on to his son and heir intact. But in order to avoid civil war, the Tsar bowed to the inevitable by agreeing to the creation of a consultative body, the Duma. Though there were widespread calls for revolution, "many Russians (also) felt as Nicholas did, facing the inevitability of change only with reluctance."

As for the imperial family, the events leading up to the signing of the October Manifesto were so dire that plans had been discussed as to the possible need to evacuate the Tsar, Tsarina, and their five children from Peterhof and send them abroad. The Grand Marshal of the Court, Count

Paul Benckendorff, admitted to Witte, however, that the five children "would be a great hindrance" should the family have to be evacuated. As it turned out, the imperial family was not evacuated. But this concern expressed by Benckendorff, a loyal court retainer and close friend of the Nicholas II, illustrates that the delicate health of the Tsarevich was already giving serious cause for concern.

Alexei was almost a year-and-a-half old when his father was compelled to sign the October Manifesto; and already at that young age, the empire Tsarevich Alexei was born to rule one day teetered on the brink of revolution.

Chapter 3.   "Their Heaviest Cross" (1906-1911)

As 1905 ended, it became evident that unless calm prevailed in the near future, the young Tsarevich would inherit an unstable crown and though "the dynasty enjoyed a reprieve," in that it had not been overthrown, there was little doubt that Nicholas II was "sitting on a throne of bayonets."

Six months after signing the October Manifesto, a historic event took place. The first Duma was installed in April 1906 with the Tsar presiding over the ceremony in the Winter Palace. Nicholas II wore his regimental uniform of the Preobrazehnsky Guards, and the ladies of the court including the Tsarina, the Dowager Empress, and Grand Duchesses wore elaborate court gowns, covered in precious jewelry. The atmosphere in the cavernous St. George's Hall was tense. The Tsar's mother and sister found certain Duma members to have been indifferent to the unfolding ceremony, with the workmen, in particular, looking angry and hateful.

Such antipathy only served to underscore in the mind of Tsarina Alexandra, the need to stay away more than ever from St. Petersburg. It did not help her confidence that a rival court emerged where the Grand Duchess Marie Pavlovna, an aunt of the Tsar, entertained lavishly in the capital and made no secret of her poor opinion about Tsarina Alexandra. But Alexandra's health also precluded her from entertaining on a large scale. In fact, during these years, the Tsarina's health had weakened to the extent that she could not accompany her husband and daughters on daily walks at Tsarskoe Selo.

The four girls, who liked to refer to themselves collectively as 'OTMA' from their first initials, continued to be raised in a sheltered environment like their only brother. They had few playmates and relied on each other for support and friendship. Like their parents, the Grand Duchesses doted on the Tsarevich. As Alexei went from being a toddler to a little boy, his impishness, so similar to his sister, Anastasia, came to the fore. He grew into a "high spirited," "lively boy full of fun." Not surprisingly, as the only son and heir, with an incurable illness, Alexei became spoilt. He was showered with toys, both simple and expensive ones from stuffed animals and musical instruments to toy trains, ships, railways, armies of tin soldiers and even a working miniature mechanical mine and factories. The young Tsarevich picked up on the fact that he was special and sensed early on that he was deferred to and given due respect for his rank and expected to be treated as such, leading to an imperious streak. When Alexei was four years hold, he had surprised the wife of the imperial family's physician, Dr. Eugene Botkin, when she greeted the Tsarevich with a bow and said, "How do you do, Your Imperial Highness?"

By way of a reply, Alexei "frowned angrily and turned away his head." Upon learning of the incident, Dr. Botkin told his wife that, "of course the Heir was angry with you. You should have bowed to him in silence, for you have no right to say anything before he himself had started to talk with you."

The Tsarevich Alexei's imperiousness was not allowed to go on indefinitely and it was eventually curbed. What did not subside, however, were concerns over his health. In fact, with each passing year, the anxieties only continued to mount thanks to the fact that Alexei was, like most boys, keen to play and be rambunctious, which, in his case, meant that accidents were prone to happen; and accidents could easily lead to serious bleeding episodes that could mean death.

Painful as it was for Tsar Nicholas to have a son with this debilitating illness, Tsarina Alexandra took Alexei's hemophilia harder. Sophie Buxhoeveden saw this first-hand and noted that, "his illness was the tragedy of her happy home life. She could never feel for an hour that he was safe." Because this was so, "the little accidents that are bound to happen to a lively child were grave dangers in his case. Just because a fall was so serious to him he seemed always to be falling."

It all amounted to a difficult life for Nicholas and Alexandra. Grand Duchess Olga Alexandrovna, the Tsar's sister, summed it up when she noted how, "the birth of a son, which should have been the happiest event in the lives of Nicky and Alicky, became their heaviest cross…"

The Tsarina, in particular, felt keenly the fact that she had given her husband and Russia a sickly heir. Though the nation did not truly know what plagued Alexei, rumors eventually abounded so that it became an accepted fact that Alexei was not healthy. Consequently, it was "most painful to the feelings of the Empress, whose maternal pride was hurt by the knowledge that the whole of Russia was commenting on it and pitying the Emperor for having an heir in such a sad state of health."

Pierre Gilliard, who later became Alexei's French tutor, summed up the situation best when he described his first meeting with the heir to the throne when the Tsarevich was eighteen months old. Of the Tsarina Alexandra, Gilliard wrote: "I could see she was transfused by the delirious joy of a mother who at last has seen her dearest wish fulfilled. She was proud and happy in the beauty of her child. The Czarevitch was certainly one of the handsomest babies one could imagine, with his lovely fair curls and his great blue-grey eyes under their fringe of long curling lashes. He had the fresh pink colour of a healthy child, and when he smiled there were two little dimples in his chubby cheeks." But then Gilliard noticed how guarded the Tsarina became over Alexei, how her maternal instincts came to the fore. "At that first meeting I saw the Czarina press the little boy to her with the convulsive movement of a mother who always seems in fear of her child's life." Tsarina Alexandra had revealed to Gilliard, "a secret apprehension so marked and poignant that I was struck at once."

Besides his parents, nurses hovered around the Tsarevich's side. Alexei grew into a lively, curious toddler whose mobility increased with each passing month which meant that he inevitably wobbled and tumbled. One such incident caused much consternation. When he was three-years-old, Alexei fell, hitting his forehead, causing his face to swell and his eyes to close. The boy's aunt, Grand Duchess Olga Alexandrovna, rushed to Tsarskoe Selo to find her nephew "in such pain, dark patches under his eyes and his little body all distorted, and the leg terribly swollen." The news perturbed his paternal grandmother, causing her to write to her son from Buckingham Palace, where the Dowager Empress was visiting her sister, Queen Alexandra: "Poor boy it is terrible, I can imagine how frightened you were; but what did he stumble against? I hope it is all over now, and that his charming little face has not suffered from it."

It was only a matter of time before another frightening attack would inflict undue pain and suffering to the Tsarevich. Because this was so and because he was her longed-for son, Alexei's mother at first was inclined to spoil him. But as he grew, efforts to reign in the child's strong will bore fruit. For one thing, Tsarina Alexandra tried to inculcate in all her children a need to be truthful and when it came to the Tsarevich, the angriest Alexandra had been on him was when she discovered young Alexei telling her a falsehood. Because she was dogged by people who were insincere, Tsarina Alexandra was determined that her son and daughters grew up to be honest. In the Tsarina's eyes, one of the best ways to keep her children immune from outside negative influences was to raise them away from St. Petersburg.

It was thus in the Neoclassical eighteenth century Alexander Palace some twenty-six miles from St. Petersburg that Tsarevich Alexei and his sisters grew up. Built by Catherine the Great for her grandson, Tsar Alexander I, the interiors of the Alexander Palace were both splendid and homely. Gold chandeliers, marble, intricately patterned parquet floors, large gilt-edged portraits of Romanov tsars and grand dukes, along with beautiful antique furniture impressed visitors in the formal rooms. In the private quarters of the family, however, simpler tastes prevailed. Chintzes and comfortable, practical furniture were used; and in Alexei's room, hung religious icons similar to the ones found in the rooms of his parents and sisters.

As Alexei grew, Nicholas and Alexandra were challenged to raise their only son in such a way as to protect him from his illness, but at the same time, they also had to educate Alexei as heir. "The combination of exalted rank and hemophilia saw to it that" Nicholas and Alexandra's only son "grew up under a degree of care rarely lavished on any child." By the time the Tsarevich turned five, two sailors, Nagorny and Derevenko, were assigned to watch over the child to try to keep him from being injured. Derevenko was especially helpful in alleviating Alexei's discomfort and pain. The boy would ask Derevenko to "warm my hands," or "lift my arm." The Tsarina's confidante, Anna Viroubova, recalled how the ever-patient Derevenko could be found "working for hours on end to give the maximum comfort to the little pain-racked limbs." The sailors also carried Alexei when he had trouble walking.

But when Alexei was well, he could be a handful. For as he grew older, Alexei was no different than any other boy his age in that he enjoyed playing and being boisterous. Despite his parents' admonitions for him to be careful, Tsarevich Alexei yearned to be allowed to play like any other boy. But there were times when he was held back and the result was predictable.

"Can't I have a bicycle," the Tsarevich begged his mother.

"Alexei, you know you can't," came the Tsarina's inevitable reply.

"Mayn't I play tennis," went another request from Alexei to his mother.

"Dear, you know you musn't."

The Tsarevich's frustrations burst forth as he cried: "Why can't other boys have everything and I nothing?"

As the years passed, Alexei's self-denial affected him. But instead of having a corrosive effect on the Tsarevich's character, it did the opposite. Alexei's illness and suffering made him sensitive to others who were mistreated or sick. The Tsarevich's empathy toward the less fortunate was reinforced by his Orthodox faith. The Tsarina Alexandra tried her best to be a good mother and took it upon herself to ensure that her son and daughters were raised to love and appreciate the Orthodox faith. The Tsarina, always a religious woman, had been a reluctant convert to Orthodoxy from Lutheranism. She took her faith seriously and for some time did not accept Nicholas's entreatics to marry him and convert. When she finally did embrace Orthodoxy and married her husband, Alexandra became a fervent adherent to her new faith. With Nicholas II equally devout, it came as no surprise that the imperial couple raised their children to have a deep-seated faith.

Tsarina Alexandra always saw Alexei as a most special gift from God. One of Alexandra's closest friends, Lili Dehn, commented how, "to the Empress, the Tsarevitch represented the direct result of prayer, the Divine condescension of God, the crowning joy of her marriage. Surely, if she manifested undue anxiety over him, she only did what all mothers have done, and will do until the end of time."

As much as she desired to keep Alexei cocooned inside the Alexander Palace, the Tsarina knew that this was not always possible. She let her son roam outdoors on the grounds of Tsarksoe Selo which was a demi-paradise. Lakes, parks with plenty of trees, grottoes, bridges, and follies all made for a beautiful setting. In warm weather, Alexei and his sisters went boating; in winter they played in the snow and helped their father shovel snow from the paths. Alexei was allowed to have a few playmates close to his age. The sons of Derevenko, his sailor bodyguard, were among them, as was the son of another physician, Dr. Derevenko, and the children of Dr. Eugene Botkin. Gleb, Botkin's son, recalled how the Tsarevich resembled his youngest sister, the boisterous Grand Duchess Anastasia. Gleb Botkin remembered that Alexei had the same "gift of noise making" and that, "he had the same shrill voice, as well as the accomplished impertinence of Anastasia."

The combination of a lively character and sickly constitution made the Tsarevich, "to whom the young boy was" his parents' "very heart's blood," a source of joy and sorrow. In recalling his childhood playmate, Gleb Botkin remembered what Alexei had been to his parents and sisters: "Everybody in the family adored and pitied him."

Not surprisingly, owing to his delicate health, educating the Tsarevich could prove challenging at times. Pierre Gilliard had admitted as much to A.A.

Mossolov, who described the Tsarevich's education as having presented "enormous difficulties. Scarcely had a course of study begun when the Cesarevitch would fall ill; the effusions of blood brought him terrible suffering; he spent whole nights groaning and begging for help that no one could give him. His malady exhausted him and set his nerves on edge; and in that state the little sufferer came back to his lessons, with everything to begin afresh." It was a near thankless task for Alexei's tutors, for, as Mossolov put it, "could this poor little unfortunate be blamed if he proved wanting in diligence and concentration?" Alexei could indeed be backwards when it came to his lessons, but this did not take away from the fact that the Tsarevich possessed a clever mind. He had a "good memory, and when he was well he worked hard to make up for lost time."

As he grew, Alexei came to resemble a combination of his parents. His once blond hair had turned dark brown, but his eyes remained a deep blue. The Tsarevich also continued to be the center of family life. As the "child of many prayers" and the favorite of his mother, Alexei could have been envied and resented by his sisters. But such was not the case. Lili Dehn, recorded that, Alexei's sisters, in fact, "adored him."

Despite his lively nature, the specter of death was never far from the Tsarevich Alexei. Gleb Botkin remembered how "because of the frequent hemorrhages caused by his illness," Alexei "had to be kept in bed for months at a time, suffering excruciating pains."

This, then, became the pattern for the imperial family. There were times when the heir felt well and appeared healthy. He took to his lessons, played, enjoyed life. And then, an attack of hemophilia felled him. The hemorrhaging started, the blood flowed. Joints stiffened. The pain, at times excruciating, became unbearable. The suffering, the heart-stopping fear, returned. The vigil began. Lessons stopped. Incessant prayers were offered up to the Almighty. Anxieties grew by leaps and bounds. The anxious mother became desperate with anguish. Could anyone, she wondered, be on the horizon who might wrought from the Almighty, extraordinary miracles to help her precious son?

Chapter 4.   Rasputin (1906-1912)

No story about Tsar Nicholas II, Tsarina Alexandra, and their only son, Tsarevich Alexei, is complete without reference to Grigory Rasputin, the controversial peasant mystic from Siberia whose influence with the last Tsarina helped to bring down the Romanov dynasty.

Born around 1870, a *moujik* or peasant in a Siberian village, Rasputin took on the role of a *staretz*, a man who renounced the world to lead a monastic life and as such was accorded respect. Consequently, when Rasputin first arrived in St. Petersburg in 1905, he was at first welcomed in religious circles. Prelates close to Nicholas and Alexandra were not opposed to the couple meeting Rasputin. Others, however, saw nothing appealing in Rasputin. Uncouth and gruff, Rasputin with his straggly beard, penetrating and hypnotic eyes, attracted and repelled people he came into contact with. As for Alexandra, according to one of her confidantes, "the Empress saw him solely with religious eyes, neither the uncouth peasant, nor the man, but the helping spirit in her hour of need."

Tsarina Alexandra, realizing that science could not help Alexei, "determined to wrest from God the miracle which science denied." In 1906, the Tsarina's prayers seemed to have been answered. In October that year, Nicholas II wrote to Peter Stolypin, his Prime Minister, of a fateful meeting: "A few days ago I received a peasant from the Tobolsk district, Grigory Rasputin…He made a remarkably strong impression both on her Majesty and on myself, so that instead of five minutes our conversation went on for more than an hour." At the end of the year, the Tsar wrote in his diary that the Montenegrin sisters, the Grand Duchesses Anastasia and Militza "spent the whole evening telling us about Grigory."

Within the year, Rasputin had performed the first of numerous 'miracles' when it came to the Tsarevich Alexei. The fall that he took when he was three which had caused his grandmother and Aunt Olga such concerns turned out to be the first incident where Rasputin's showed his extraordinary and baffling ability to 'cure' Alexei's hemophilia attacks. Olga Alexandrovna remembered how useless the doctors had been at this instance. The Tsarina, desperate about her son's health, sent for Rasputin who arrived late into the night. He prayed at the foot of Alexei's bed. By the next morning, Olga could not believe her eyes. "The little boy was not just alive – but well. He was sitting up in bed, the fever gone, the eyes clear and bright, not a sign of any swelling on his leg." Rasputin's prayers had a miraculous effect. Olga, who was not an unstinting admirer of Rasputin, admitted that she could not count how many times this had happened. And when the Grand Duchess spoke to Professor Feodorov, an eminent physician who took care of the Tsarevich, he confessed that Rasputin had some kind of positive, unexplainable effect when it came to 'curing' Alexei.

As Rasputin's closeness to the imperial family and his seemingly growing influence with the Tsarina became apparent, he began to garner opposition. Two factions emerged in Russia where Rasputin was concerned: his supporters and his detractors. When it came to Tsarina Alexandra, Rasputin had an indisputable champion. His unexplainable and uncanny ability to 'heal' the Tsarevich from his hemophilia attacks were the source of Alexandra's unswerving belief in him. She was not the only one astounded by Rasputin's 'powers' to heal. Even his detractors conceded that the *staretz* had this strange, inexplicable ability. A.A. Mossolov, who was not an admirer of Rasputin, conceded that, "Rasputin had incontestable success in the field of healing; I have no idea how he managed it."

The Tsarina became convinced of Rasputin's indispensability. Time and again he appeared to cure Alexei from his hemophilia attacks. To the distraught mother, they were nothing short of miracles. Even the heir's doctors were baffled as to how these 'cures' could occur. And if such eminent men of science were dumbfounded, then what else could one believe but that Rasputin had been sent by the Almighty – so went the thinking of Tsarina Alexandra. After seeing such astonishing feats when it came to 'curing' Alexei's hemophilia attacks, the Tsarina became a genuine believer in Rasputin's abilities to heal. She "sincerely thought that this common peasant, by reason of his ignorance, would be better able than a more cultured person to come into touch with the Almighty, founding her belief on the words of the Gospel, that He 'revealed himself to simple and ignorant people..'" According to Anna Viroubova, "the Imperial Family firmly believed that they owed much of Alexei's improving health to the prayers of Rasputine. Alexei himself believed it."

After Alexei turned twelve, there appeared to be an improvement in his health. The hemophilia attacks became fewer. The Tsarina had been told by Rasputin a few years before that when the Tsarevich turned twelve he would begin to get better and that by the time he became a man, Alexei would be well. When the Tsar and Tsarina did, indeed, see an improvement in their son, "they believed that the healing hand of God had wrought the cure, and that it was in answer to the supplication of one whose spirit was able to rise in higher flight than theirs or any other's." Alexei was getting better. He believed this; and his parents did too. Rasputin thus became indispensable to the Tsarina.

The Tsarina explained to N.P. Sabline, an officer on the imperial yacht, *Standart*, her views on Rasputin, telling Sabline that, "there are people, whose prayers have a particular force because of their ascetic way of life, and at last declared that in Russia there was such a man, that it was Rasputin." Sabline ascribed "her blind faith in Rasputin, as indeed the Emperor's, to their boundless love for the Heir, who was suffering from an illness pronounced incurable by the doctors."

The Tsarevich Alexei bore his illness and hemophilia attacks with great patience, but it was difficult for his parents to see him suffer. The Tsar and Tsarina were desperate to find ways of alleviating their son's pain whenever the hemophilia attacks felled him. They refused the use of morphine on Alexei due to its highly addicting effects. Rasputin's appearance on the scene was therefore more than welcomed. To the Tsarina, his arrival at court appeared to be the answer to her prayers when it came to help for her ailing son.

How Rasputin appeared to be able to calm the hemophilia attacks of the Tsarevich and seemingly be able to stop them remained a great mystery to the contemporaries of Tsar Nicholas and Tsarina Alexandra. Alexei's doctors, eminent men of science were baffled. Lacking in answers, some thought this miraculous ability stemmed from the man's forceful personality and ability to hypnotize.

When Lili Dehn met Rasputin for the first time, she was, "instantly struck by his uncanny appearance. At first glance, he appeared to be a typical peasant from the frozen North, but his eyes held mine, those shining steel-like eyes which seemed to read one's inmost thoughts." Rasputin also "possessed hypnotic and spiritual forces, he believed in himself and made others do so."

When Prince Felix Yussopov who belonged to Russia's wealthiest family, first met Rasputin in 1909, he found the peasant from Siberia irritatingly self-assured and "seemed to be constantly watching the person he was talking to." There was also "something really extraordinary about his peasant face" and "his glance was both piercing and sullen" - and the impression Felix had of Rasputin's eyes "was that of being pierced with needles rather than of merely being looked at." Peter Stolypin, Russia's Prime Minister, almost succumbed to Rasputin's attempt to hypnotize him, and told Yussopov of the fact; that Rasputin "was just beginning to gain ascendancy over me when I managed to regain control of myself and, cutting him short, bluntly told him he was completely in my power."

To the Tsarina Alexandra, what anyone thought of Rasputin made no difference to her opinion. All that mattered was that he could help her son like no one could. She had seen it with her own eyes what the Almighty could do through Rasputin who once told her: "Believe in the power of my prayers; believe in my help and your son will live!"

Pierre Gilliard saw what was happening within the confines of Tsarskoe Selo and wrote for posterity that: "Rasputin had realised the state of mind of the despairing mother who was broken down by the strain of her struggle and seemed to have touched the limit of human suffering. He knew how to extract the fullest advantage from it" – and so became the one person who could not be barred from the imperial family.

Rasputin may have appeared to have been a religious *moujik* to the Tsarina, a genuine *staretz*, but he soon showed to others, another unsavory side to him which became widely known. He was a womanizer whose loose ways set off unrestrained gossip in St. Petersburg, gossip that had a corrosive effect of damaging the imperial couple, especially the Tsarina.

Grand Duchess Olga, Nicholas II's sister, who met Rasputin several times, left an account which shows the contradictions found in the man. When she first saw him, Olga "felt that gentleness and warmth radiated from him," and that all of the Tsar and Tsarina's children "seemed to like him." Olga watched as Rasputin and Alexei prayed in the boy's room in front of the religious icons hanging there. The Grand Duchess noted how, "the child stood very still by the side of that giant, whose head was bowed. I knew he was praying. It was all most impressive. I also knew that my little nephew had joined him in prayer. I really cannot describe it – but I was conscious of the man's utter sincerity." But as she came to know the *staretz* more, Olga also went on to say that though she allowed Rasputin his sincerity, "I could never bring myself to like him." She found Rasputin's prying, impertinent questions about her personal life disturbing

With Rasputin's closeness to the imperial couple a well-known fact, plus stories of his womanizing, it was inevitable that salacious rumors about him and the Tsarina circulated throughout the capital and other parts of Russia. Stories about

Rasputin's reputed insolent behavior toward the imperial couple also made the rounds of St. Petersburg. Grand Duchess Olga Alexandrovna, who was close to Nicholas and Alexandra, absolutely refuted the gossip about Rasputin and the imperial family. Olga was adamant that such insolent behavior "would never have been tolerated for an instant." Rasputin, who called the Tsar and Tsarina *batushka* and *matushka*, 'little father' and 'little mother,' did not know much about etiquette, but according to Grand Duchess Olga, he "was always respectful." But the gossip about Rasputin grew with the years. It was even said that the Tsarina was unfaithful to the Tsar because of her friendship with the notorious *moujik*. Lili Dehn, Alexandra's close friend, refuted this accusation, stating that, "Rasputin's influence over the Empress was purely mystical." Dehn went further, stating that, "there may have been some truth that Rasputin's private life was not all that it should have been, but I assert most solemnly that we never saw the slightest trace of impropriety in word, manner or behaviour when he was with us at Tsarskoe Selo." Nevertheless, unlike Anna Viroubova, who was a devotee of Rasputin, Dehn was under no illusions about the man's behavior outside of Tsarskoe Selo and understood the harm his association with the Tsarina was causing.

By this time, no one, not even the Tsar, who eventually came to have misgivings about Rasputin, could convince Tsarina Alexandra to cut off any association with the *staretz*. Warnings about Rasputin from the Church and family members fell on deaf ears when it came to the Tsarina. She never forgave Stolypin for placing Rasputin in 1911 under police investigation and banishing him. Stolypin's attempts to keep Rasputin away from court did not last. In September of 1911, Stolypin was assassinated by a revolutionary in Kiev in front of the Tsar and his two eldest daughters, Olga and Tatiana. The assassination meant that an implacable enemy of Rasputin had been removed, and soon the *staretz* was back in St. Petersburg.

The crisis surrounding Rasputin and the Tsarina took a turn for the worse. It created friction at court as those close to the Tsar and Tsarina took opposing sides. Anna Viroubova remained unswerving in her devotion to the *staretz*. Dr. Botkin, on the other hand, took an immense dislike to Rasputin. Botkin's son, Gleb, wrote that when it came to his father, "because of his being sincerely devoted to Their Majesties, he regarded their attachment to Rasputin as being a fatal mistake."

The Tsarina's unshakable faith in Rasputin was encapsulated in the one sentence which she invariably uttered when doubts about the man were cast: "I believe in Rasputin." This belief was tied to the fate of the Tsarevich, which meant that, "the nursery was the centre of all Russia's troubles."

By 1912, the rumors about Rasputin and his supposed nefarious influence on the Tsar and Tsarina had reached a point that Nicholas II's mother, the Dowager Empress Marie Feodorovna, expressed her concerns to Mikhail Rodzianko, President of the Duma, telling him, that when she first heard of the Rasputin story, "I was absolutely aghast. It is terrible, terrible." Even the Grand Duchesses Anastasia and Militza, one-time champions of Rasputin, warned the Tsarina about him. She reacted by cutting ties with them.

If anyone thought that there was still hope that the Tsarina might give up on Rasputin, they were to be sorely mistaken; for one harrowing event involving Tsarevich Alexei in 1912 would cement in the Tsarina's mind, Rasputin's reputation as miracle worker who was the only one who could save her son from certain death.

ILLUSTRATIONS

Alexei Nikolaevich, Tsarevich of Russia (1904-1918) (public domain)

Tsarina Alexandra with her only son, Tsarevich Alexei on board the imperial yacht, the *Standart*.
(Beinecke Rare Book and Manuscript Library, Yale University)

Russian Imperial Family, c. 1913-14. Back row (left to right): Grand Duchess Marie (sitting), Grand Duchess Olga and Grand Duchess Tatiana. Center: Tsarina Alexandra, Tsar Nicholas II, Grand Duchess Anastasia. Foreground: Tsarevich Alexei (public domain)

The front entrance of the Alexander Palace,
Tsarskoe Selo (author collection)

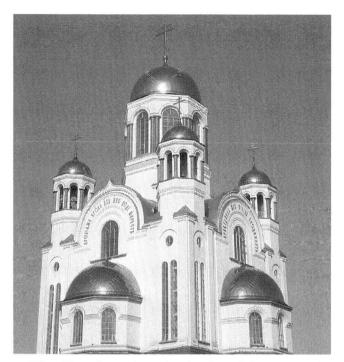

The Church on the Blood, Ekaterinburg, Russia, the site of the execution of the Romanovs. (Pixabay)

Chapter 5. Spala (1912) & Tercentenary Celebrations (1913)

B y the time he had reached his ninth year, Tsarevich Alexei had grown into a handsome youth, possessing his mother's blue-grey eyes. Pierre Gilliard noted that Alexei had "a long, finely-chiselled face, delicate features, auburn hair with a coppery glint in it." As far as his intelligence and personality, the Tsarevich "had very quick wits and a keen and penetrating mind." Alexei sometimes surprised Gilliard "with questions beyond his years which bore witness to a delicate and intuitive spirit." The French tutor wrote of Alexei: "He thoroughly enjoyed life – when it let him – and was a happy, romping boy." Gilliard also saw how Alexei "was making a real effort to control his impulsive and turbulent nature, which had unfortunately caused serious accidents."

When the Tsarevich was well, he brought laughter to those around him. During a visit to Smolensk in 1912, at a tea given by the ladies of the town, Alexei got into mischief. The Tsar recounted what happened to his mother, saying that, "Alexei got hold of a glass of champagne and drank it unnoticed, after which he became rather gay and began to entertain the ladies, to our great surprise."

It was in this happy state of good health and good humor surrounding Alexei that Nicholas and Alexandra and their children made their way to their Polish hunting estate in Spala in the autumn of 1912. All seemed well upon their arrival, but trouble soon set in. Alexei had injured himself again, this time by jumping into a boat and hitting his leg. The Tsarina sent a telegram to her close friend, Anna Viroubova, summoning her to join the worried family. Anna duly arrived and found the family ensconced in a large, damp, wooden villa surrounded by thick forests. Even here, the family could not escape the presence of bodyguards and the atmosphere was one of gloom. Nevertheless, the hunting was exceptional with stags and huge bison roaming the forests. The Tsar continued to entertain his guests who had come to join him for the hunting while he and the Tsarina tried to keep news of Alexei's illness hidden from their guests.

One day, in an attempt to buoy her son's spirits, the Tsarina took Alexei on a carriage ride with Anna. The Tsarevich's condition worsened during the ride, prompting his mother to rush back to the villa. From then on, Alexei suffered agonies, for this injury had turned out to be the worst hemophilia attack to date. The boy was hemorrhaging, his thigh had swelled and the blood continued to wreak havoc inside Alexei's body, attacking his bones, abdomen, and tissues. The doctors could do nothing. The parents prayed desperately. The death agony had begun.

Anna, who was privy to all the pitiful scenes, recalled how, "the next weeks were endless torment to the boy and to all of us who had to listen to his constant cries of pain. For fully eleven days these dreadful sounds filled the corridors outside his room, and those of us who were obliged to approach had often to stop our ears with our hands in order to go about our duties."

The cries of the sick child were loud at first, but as he grew weaker and lost strength, Alexei's cries turned hoarser and became moans. The sailor Derevenko carried the ailing Tsarevich for hours when the child thought this might ease his pain. But often Alexei lay in his bed, "growing thinner and more deathlike every day, as the weakness increased, his great eyes looking like coals in his little, wan, drawn face."

Watching her beloved son suffer such torturous pain was unbearable for Tsarina Alexandra. She nursed him as best as she could, hardly leaving his side. As for the Tsar, Alexei's sufferings became too much. His son's face "was absolutely bloodless, drawn and seamed with suffering, while his almost expressionless eyes rolled back in his head." When the distraught father entered the Tsarevich's room, "seeing his boy in this agony and hearing faint screams of pain," Nicholas's courage "completely gave way and he rushed, weeping bitterly, to his study." Alexei's agonies continued endlessly. Suffering from a high fever, delirium soon set in. But in a moment of lucidity, Alexei was so convinced that he was not long for this world that he told his poor mother, "when I am dead, build me a little monument of stones in the wood."

In a letter to his mother, the Tsar wrote movingly of what Alexei had to endure. "The poor darling suffered intensely, the pains came in spasms and recurred every quarter of an hour." At one point, wrote Nicholas of his son that, "he hardly slept at all, had not even the strength to cry, just moaned and kept repeating: 'O Lord, have mercy upon me.'"

A.A. Mossolov wrote of the terror that gripped the Tsar and Tsarina when it came to Alexei: "The anxiety of his mother and father was beyond description." Nicholas and Alexandra's anxieties soon plunged to despair. The doctors told the Tsarina, "they could do nothing more." Alexei was dying. Bulletins broke the news to the nation of the Tsarevich's dire state. Peasants from the surrounding area around Spala came to the estate to pray for the dying boy. They stood next to the Tsar's entourage in a tent hastily prepared on the grounds as a chapel. Another bulletin was prepared. It stated that the Tsarevich had died. It was set to be released soon after Alexei's death. One of the Romanov grand dukes recorded in his diary: "There was a bulletin in the *Evening Times* about the illness of the Tsarevich. He is the Emperor's only son! May God protect him!"

In desperation, Tsarina Alexandra resorted to the man who had helped heal Alexei before, the one man who seemed to be able to get God to hear her prayers. A telegram was sent from Spala to

Pokrovske, in Siberia where Rasputin was. Alexandra begged for Rasputin to pray for Alexei. His reply came: "The little one will not die."

Mossolov recalled how a telegram had arrived at Spala from Rasputin stating that the Tsarevich should not be "allowed to be martyred by the doctors." The very next day, the doctors went in search of Mossolov. When they found him, the first words they said to him were, "the haemorrhage has stopped."

Almost as if on cue, the Tsarevich miraculously improved soon after Rasputin's telegram arrived at Spala. The child had been snatched from the jaws of death. The doctors were stunned and at a loss as to how this miraculous recovery could take place so suddenly. Rasputin had done the unbelievable again. The Tsarevich Alexei had been saved. And this time Rasputin was nowhere near Alexei, such was the power of prayer he seemed to have.

When Alexei had shown signs of recovery, the imperial doctors issued a bulletin to the public explaining in some detail what the boy had to endure, though the word 'hemophilia' was never mentioned. There were descriptions of "an abdominal hemorrhage" and of a "new hemorrhage which "covered a much larger area, that is: the whole left iliac region and the whole lumbar region of that side, while its inside limit stretched a little over the middle line of the stomach." The bulletin went on to add that, "the results of such widespread haemorrhaging are a significant anemia, which sometimes needs considerable time to cure completely, as well as prolonged difficulty with the free use of the leg, on the side where the hematoma was, as a result of the bent hip muscle and surrounding tissues having been flooded with blood, and also from the prolonged pressure of the swelling on the nerve."

Tsar Nicholas wrote to his mother of his relief that Alexei had survived this latest, most traumatic hemophilia attack, saying that, "my heart [is] filled with gratitude to the Lord for his mercy in granting us the beginning of dear Alexey's recovery." As for the Tsarina, her lady-in-waiting, Sophie Buxhoeveden summed up what happened: "After 1912, when, as she believed, he had saved the Cesarevitch's life at Spala, the Empress pinned all her faith in him. She would not entertain a doubt as to his sanctity."

Tsarevich Alexei's recovery from his near-fatal hemophilia attack at Spala was a protracted one. But he was able to participate in some of the important events associated with a significant anniversary in 1913: the Tercentenary celebrations commemorating three hundred years of the reign of the Romanov dynasty. It was an important anniversary for the dynasty and for a monarch who unique among his peers. The journalist, diplomat, and author, R.H. Bruce Lockhart, wrote that, "the Tsar of all the Russians occupied a position unlike that of any ruler of the world. The divine right of Kings of the Stuart epoch was a small thing compared with the divine right of Emperors in the Russia of 1913."

The official celebrations, which were "intended to be a national rejoicing," began in St. Petersburg with a religious service of thanksgiving in Our Lady of Kazan Cathedral. Upon arriving at the cathedral, the President of the Duma, Mikhail Rodzianko, learned that Rasputin, dressed magnificently in a crimson tunic, was present. Rodzianko was determined to eject Rasputin out of the cathedral. An altercation between the two forceful men ensued. Rodzianko, the powerfully built Duma leader, found the infamous *moujik* possessed of a strange personality, recounting how, "I felt myself confronted by an unknown power of tremendous force." The confrontation compelled Rodzianko to become possessed "of an almost animal fury, the blood rushed to my heart, and I realized I was working myself into a state of absolute frenzy."

"Clear out, you vile heretic," said Rodzianko to Rasputin, "there is no place for you in this sacred house!"

"I was invited here at the wish of persons more highly placed than you," replied Rasputin in an insolent manner.

It was clear that the Tsar and Tsarina had granted Rasputin an invitation. Rodzianko was nevertheless determined to eject Rasputin and succeeded in doing so.

When the imperial family arrived at the cathedral, it was clear that the heir to the throne was not in the best of health. In his ninth year, Alexei did not walk into the church but was carried in by a Cossack.

The Tercentenary celebrations in the capital marked the first major appearance Tsar Nicholas II and Tsarina Alexandra had made in St. Petersburg in a decade. Though their subjects were out in the streets to see them, as they entered the Kazan Cathedral, the imperial family was greeted by "thin crowds and even sparser applause … there were no great ovations: not for the tsar or his heir; not for the tsarina or the dowager empress or for the four young grand duchesses." This lack of enthusiasm was detected by Anna Viroubova during a performance at the Mariinsky Theater where Glinka's, *A Life for the Tsar*, was performed to great applause. "But for all that," wrote Viroubova, "I felt that there was in the brilliant audience little real enthusiasm, little real loyalty."

For several days, parties and balls were given in honor of the Romanov Tercentenary. Among the imperial family, the ones who relished these festivities were Alexei's two eldest sisters, Olga and Tatiana, who took part with enthusiasm in the court life in the capital. For the Tsar and Tsarina's eldest child, Grand Duchess Olga Nikolaevna, the Tercentenary celebrations proved a special time. The eighteen-year-old made her St. Petersburg debut in a formal dance held at the Assembly of Nobles where her poise and good nature charmed one and all. The Tsarina Alexandra's appearances, however, were noted for their awkwardness. The Tsarina, still naturally shy, serious, and introspective, was also well aware of the calumnies being heaped upon her and Rasputin. Because of all this, she limited as much as she could, her appearances in the capital. Alexandra clearly felt uncomfortable amidst all the attention and appeared pained by having to mingle with St. Petersburg society. At the Mariinsky, Alexandra could not even stay for the entire performance by the corps de ballet. Pale and nervous, she excused herself and left early. The Tsarina was clearly not well. No one could fathom the trials and tribulations Tsarina Alexandra had gone through seeing her son at death's door in Spala. Alexei's latest, most serious hemophilia attack had taken its toll on Alexandra. She had aged, and no longer showed signs of the beauty she had possessed as a young woman when she first married Nicholas. The Tsarina admitted to Anna Viroubova that, "I was so happy then, so well and strong. Now I am a wreck."

Exhausted by the rounds of festivities in the capital, Tsarina Alexandra welcomed the chance later that year, to visit with her family, the hinterlands of Russia, as they cruised down the Volga River. The Tsar and Tsarina were impressed by the seeming devotion of the peasants who cheered them. But overall, most of those who had come out to see their sovereigns and their children during all the Tercentenary celebrations were moved more by curiosity than great feelings of love and affection. The gulf between the imperial couple and their subjects had not been closed. The coming years would see whether that breach would become even wider.

CHAPTER 6.   THE WAR
YEARS (1914-1917)

As the years went by, the Alexander Palace at Tsarskoe Selo continued to be the main the home of Tsar Nicholas and Tsarina Alexandra. But parts of the year were also spent cloistered away at the Lower Dacha in Peterhof; and in parts of the summer, the imperial family, boarded the imperial yacht, *Standart*, and went on a leisurely cruise off the Finnish skerries. The imperial family also cherished their stay at Livadia in the Crimea. Here, in an Italianate palace with views over the Black Sea, the family went for walks, rides in the bucolic countryside, and swam. In April, the imperial family participated in the White Flower Festival where they collected money to help support tubercular patients, many of whom convalesced in the Crimea. Alexei, dressed in his sailor uniform eagerly participated in the charity bazaars organized by his mother. Alexei's sisters, the Tsar, and the court all did their part as well to help raise funds. The Tsarina was a driving force in helping to raise money for the victims of tuberculosis. She also visited patients in the sanitoriums around the vicinity of Livadia, and encouraged her daughters to do the same, telling Sophie Buxhoeveden that, "they should realise the sadness underneath all this beauty."

By this time, the Grand Duchesses had grown into well-mannered young women with distinct personalities, thoroughly Russian to the core. Olga was sensitive and spiritual; Tatiana, elegant and reticent; Marie, artistic and easy-going; Anastasia, fearless and impish. They continued to be devoted to their only brother, who reciprocated their loyal affection.

A plethora of articles and postcards on the Tsar, Tsarina, and their children gave the public, abroad and within Russia, some idea of their domestic and political lives – but only just. And so, the family very much remained a mystery to their subjects and to those outside of Russia. Only a small coterie of intimates truly knew them; and this included other members of the Romanov family. For with the exception of the Tsar's mother; his two sisters, the Grand Duchesses Olga and Xenia; and his brother-in-law, Sandro (Xenia's husband), none of the other Romanovs saw much of Nicholas and Alexandra and their family. Faithful retainers like Dr. Botkin, Anna Viroubova, Sophie Buxhoeveden, and Pierre Gilliard knew the family much better.

Gilliard accompanied the family to Livadia in the spring of 1914 and noted how, after Spala, Alexei's health had finally improved; "he had grown a good deal, and he looked so well that we were all in high spirits." Being in the Crimea no doubt helped to lift everyone's spirits. Here, in this temperate part of Russia with its lush vegetation and profusion of fragrant flowers, the family enjoyed a tranquil life. Livadia Palace, with its views over the Black Sea, was the ideal home for the close-knit family. Though they did very little formal entertaining, the imperial family ended up seeing more people at Livadia than at Tsarskoe Selo, thanks in part to the active charitable endeavors that Tsarina Alexandra pursued as her health permitted. As a general rule, however, Tsarina Alexandra's health continued to weaken. Pains from sciatica and what she was certain were heart problems rendered Alexandra at times a semi-invalid. She would rest and recline on a sofa in her favorite room, the Mauve Boudoir, at the Alexander Palace, or on a balcony at Livadia. Outdoors, on days when she felt especially weak, the Tsarina would be wheeled around by her attendants or daughters to enjoy the fresh air. Of the numerous health issues plaguing the Tsarina, it was her nerves that clearly affected her, due in large part to her anxieties over her son's hemophilia. This, added to Alexandra's continuing reliance on Rasputin, made for a potent mix that could unnerve the Tsar, prompting him to admit, "I prefer to have a hundred Rasputins around me rather than be obliged to endure perpetual scenes."

The negative impact Rasputin was having on the reputation of the Tsar and especially the Tsarina, continued to build. The Orthodox Church had come to oppose him; and the Duma attacked him. A Duma member, Vladimir Purishkevich, had even declared in dramatic fashion, "I would gladly sacrifice myself to kill that scoundrel!"

The Tsar eventually did concede that public opinion needed to be heeded and so managed to get Rasputin to return to his Siberian village, Pokrovskoe. But before he left for Siberia, Rasputin had warned the Tsar and Tsarina: "If you forsake me, you'll lose your son and your crown within six months."

The first six months of 1914 were the last time Nicholas and Alexandra and their children were to feel any semblance of normalcy in their family life. Alexei continued to progress and received a charming spaniel named, 'Joy.' In June, Nicholas and Alexandra and their children sailed to Constanza, the Romanian port city on the Black Sea to visit the country's king, Carol I and his family. An underlying reason for the visit was to see if an engagement might occur between the Tsar and Tsarina's eldest child, Grand Duchess Olga and the second in line to the Romanian throne, Prince Carol, son of Crown Prince Ferdinand and Crown Princess Marie. The Crown Princess, a first cousin of the Tsarina, thought young Alexei to have been "very handsome but [a] somewhat spoilt child" who nevertheless "accepted with perfect good grace" the overtures of little Princess Ileana of Romania to be her companion. As for the Tsarina, Crown Princess Marie found her cousin, "making brave efforts to be as gracious as possible, but it did not come easily to her and her face was very flushed." By the end of the trip, nothing had transpired between Olga and

Carol. She was not to make her future in Romania but stay in her beloved Russia.

Not long after the Constanza visit, the imperial family sailed on the *Standart* and anchored off Finland. During this trip, the Tsarevich had again hurt himself, twisting his ankle. He began to hemorrhage and became bedridden. The Tsarina took to ministering to him as she always did when Alexei suffered from a hemophilia attack. Then, on June 28, 1914, news reached the Tsar and Tsarina onboard the *Standart* that Archduke Franz Ferdinand, heir to the Austro-Hungarian throne, and his wife, were assassinated in Sarajevo. Shocking as that was, the news the next day that an attempt on Rasputin's life had taken place, shook the Tsarina even more. For a fortnight, Rasputin lay seriously ill but eventually recovered.

Throughout July, the crisis grew increasingly alarming over the repercussions concerning the Sarajevo assassinations so that before the month was out, the Austro-Hungarian empire had presented Serbia with an ultimatum that pointed to war. Serbia did not hesitate to look to Russia, protector of the Slavic peoples, for support. Russia felt compelled to support Serbia. The other

European alliances soon came into play. Before long, a European conflagration had erupted. World War I had begun.

In the capital, the Tsar appeared on the balcony of the Winter Palace and in a strong, resonant voice, declared the start of hostilities. Nicholas II proclaimed to the hushed throngs below him that: "The great wave of patriotism and loyalty to the Throne which has swept our native land is to me…a token that our great Mother Russia will carry on that war, sent us as a visitation by God…"

The Tsarina and her daughters had accompanied the Tsar, but Alexei was left at Peterhof, recuperating, "weeping in disappointment." Alexei had missed seeing first-hand, a moving spectacle, as cheering crowds shouted, "*Batiushka, Batiushka*, lead us to victory!" After the Tsar declared the start of the war, the family made their way to Moscow so that the Tsar could make the same proclamation there. Pierre Gilliard noted how the Tsar and Tsarina were "in despair" because their son might not be well enough to attend the ceremony in the cathedral in Moscow. "It is always the same," recorded Gilliard, "when he [Alexei] is supposed to appear in public.

You can be practically certain that some complication will prevent it. Fate seems to pursue him."

This particularly time, however, the Tsarevich did manage to appear in public and attended the religious ceremony at the cathedral in Moscow. His leg still stiff from his recent hemophilia attack, Alexei was carried in the arms of a Cossack. Tsarina Alexandra feared that there would be talk that the heir was permanently lame because nearly every time Alexei had to appear with his family at a formal event, he was inevitably carried in the arms of a soldier.

The presence of the Tsar and his family during a time of national significance excited the inhabitants of Moscow. When Gilliard and Alexei went out for a drive, their car encountered traffic and came almost to a standstill. The peasants and other ordinary folk recognized Alexei and soon a loud shout of, "The Heir! ... the Heir!" could be heard. The crowd surrounding the car went into a near frenzy emboldening some women to thrust their hands into the car's open windows. "I've touched him! ... I've touched the Heir!" came the shrieks of excitement from the crowd.

In the heady days after mobilization had been declared, crowds sang and cheered all over Russia. Support for the cause, for Russia, and for the Tsar was widespread. Tsarina Alexandra, however, was not so enthused. "It will be a terrible, monstrous struggle," she confided to Sophie Buxhoevden, "humanity is about to pass through ghastly sufferings."

Like the Tsarina, Rasputin was also of the opinion that war would bring rivers of blood. He wrote to the Tsar, saying, "a menacing cloud is over Russia … Thou art the Tsar Father of the People don't allow the madmen to triumph and destroy themselves and the People." Rasputin ended the letter with dire words, "Terrible is the destruction and without end the grief."

It did not take long for Rasputin's ominous warnings to appear. In the first month of the war, at the Battle of Tannenberg, the Germans inflicted on the Russians a great defeat which saw the loss of more than 100,000 Russian soldiers and the capture of another 90,000.

The supreme command of the Russian forces fell to the Tsar's kin, Grand Duke Nicholas, or Nikolasha, as he was referred to among the

Romanovs. The field headquarters from which Nikolasha exercised his authority was *Stavka*, which, in the summer of 1915, had relocated to Mogilev on the Dnieper River. The Tsar made periodic visits to *Stavka* to immerse himself in the war effort. Nikolasha was no friend of Rasputin's and Alexandra was well aware of it. When Rasputin requested to go to the front to bless the troops, the furious Grand Duke telegraphed back: "Do come! I will hang you!"

Alexandra never forgave Nikolasha for his hatred of Rasputin. She urged her husband to remove the Grand Duke from his post. When Warsaw fell in August 1915, Nicholas II took the fateful step of relieving the popular Nikolasha of his post and assuming it himself, this despite the protests of ministers who feared that should Russia suffer more significant military losses, the blame would be laid squarely at the Tsar's feet. It was risky move on Nicholas's part. The losses of the Russian army to this point had already been disheartening: nearly 1.5 million soldiers had been wounded or killed and nearly another million were prisoners of war. The Tsar's decision to relieve Nikolasha of his command was not popular with segments of the population. "Toward this step," wrote the Tsar's cousin, Grand Duchess Marie, "it was said he was being urged by the Empress and by Rasputin, who hated the Grand Duke Nicholas, then commanding, and suspected him of overweening ambitions."

While the Tsar busied himself with military matters, the Tsarina and her two eldest daughters, Olga and Tatiana, trained to be nurses. Alexandra, when her health permitted, was an active nurse, assisting in the operating rooms. She established a hospital for convalescing soldiers at Tsarskoe Selo and visited other military hospitals.

The Tsar and Tsarina decided that despite the delicate health of their son, it was important that he be immersed in the war effort. Alexei, like his father, was fond of the army. In the autumn of 1915, the Tsar took his eleven-year-old son with him to *Stavka*. It was a calculated move. Nicholas II hoped that, "the appearance of the Heir at his side, symbolizing the future, would further bolster" the low spirits of Russia's troops. The Tsar had also hoped that the intense masculine atmosphere found at Stavka would be a positive antidote to the sometimes suffocating isolation Alexei had to put up at home where a strong feminine influence, starting with his mother, was unavoidable.

The Tsarevich could not always be with his father at *Stavka* and when this did occur, Alexei wrote to Nicholas II, his letters peppered with references to the military which Alexei loved:

Dear Papa

> *Yesterday we played at war. I took the enemy trench in one moment but was immediately thrown back and taken prisoner. But at that very second I broke away and scrammed! My fortifications remained. I feel well How is your health? Write to me! A big kiss. May God protect you!*

Your loving Alexei

Whenever Tsarevich Alexei visited *Stavka* with the Tsar, he never neglected to write to his mother, whose anxieties over his health never abated. In one letter, Alexei wrote: "Dear Mama I missed you a lot …. In the evening I prayed for you (+ many times) …. May God protect you. Your Alexei." In another letter months later from *Stavka*, Alexei told his mother, "Dearest darling Mama …. I'm going to have lunch with everyone. I want to devour like 100 wolves!!! … God + protect you and my sisters! …. Your son and brother."

The Tsarevich's visits to *Stavka* were beneficial to him and to all who met the heir. He made friends with the generals and played with the peasant boys. Alexei, dressed in the uniform of a private, accompanied the Tsar on visits to Russian troops at the front. The Tsarevich grew closer to his father. They shared a room together at *Stavka*, a small cot having been placed near the Tsar's bed. Nicholas II wrote to his wife about life there with Alexei in October 1915:

> *The Little One's presence takes up part of my time, too, for which, of course, I am not sorry. His company gives life and light to all of us, including the foreigners. It is very cosy, sleeping side by side. I have said prayers with him every night since we were in the train; he says*

his prayers too fast, and it is difficult to stop him. He was tremendously pleased with the review; he followed me, and stood the whole time while the troops were marching past, which was splendid. I shall never forget this review. The weather was excellent and the general impression astounding. Life here goes on as usual. Alexey lunched in his room with M. Gilliard only on the first day, after that he begged hard to lunch with all of us. He sits on my left hand, and behaves well, but sometimes he becomes inordinately gay and noisy, especially when I am talking with the others in the drawing-room. In any case it is pleasant for them, and makes them smile.

Before evening sets in, we go out in the car (in the morning he plays in the garden) either into the woods or on the bank of the river, where we light a fire and I walk about near-by.

Nicholas II and Tsarevich Alexei's special bond was cemented at *Stavka*. Count Benckendorff summed up the Tsar's hopes for his son, noting that, "the Heir-Apparent – the little Grand Duke – was the especial object of his [Nicholas II] affection. His tardy birth, the poor state of his health, made him the idol of his parents. I often heard the Emperor say, in times of trouble during his reign, that he would accept all sufferings if he could leave Russia in order to prepare his son an easy and a happy reign."

Of course, never far from the Tsar's thoughts was the huge shadow of hemophilia. In one letter to the Tsarina from *Stavka*, Nicholas wrote that, "Baby played the fool, pretended to fall off his chair, and hurt his left arm … it did not hurt afterwards, but swelled up instead. So he slept very restlessly, kept on sitting up in bed, groaning, calling for you, and talking to me. Every few minutes he fell off to sleep again – this went on hourly until four o'clock … Thank God it is all over to-day – except for paleness and a slight bleeding at the nose."

Another hemophilia incident in December 1915 proved nearly fatal for the heir. A nosebleed led to a serious attack, prompting the Tsar to return with Alexei to Tsarskoe Selo. Pierre Gilliard recorded how the train journey back "was particularly harrowing" and that "I thought the end had come."

By the time the Tsar and Alexei had arrived back home to Tsarskoe Selo, it was evident that the child was again at death's door. Anna Viroubova recalled how she could "never forget the anguish of mind with which the poor mother awaited the arrival of her sick, perhaps dying child. Nor can I ever forget the waxen, grave-like pallor of the little pointed face" of Alexei as he was carefully carried back to his room. Alexei's suffering, Viroubova recorded, was evident, "for above the blood-soaked bandages his large blue eyes gazed at us with pathos unspeakable, and it seemed to all around the bed that the last hour of the unhappy child was at hand." The doctors tried everything to stop the bleeding, but to no avail. In desperation, the Tsarina called for Rasputin, who was back in St. Petersburg. Upon arriving at Alexei's room, Rasputin made the sign of the cross over the child's bed and said to the Tsar and Tsarina, kneeling in prayer: "Don't be alarmed. Nothing will happen."

And sure enough, the next day, the Tsarevich was better. Alexei's doctors could not explain the cure and did not even attempt to do so. The recovery had been so rapid that the Tsar was able to leave for *Stavka* again. "Alexei is recovering," wrote Tsar Nicholas to his mother, "and will probably get up in a few days. It is very sad going without him."

Earlier in the year Rasputin had again performed another extraordinary 'miracle' when the Tsarina's friend, Anna Viroubova, was critically injured in a train accident. Rasputin rushed to Anna's bedside and prayed with great intensity while the Tsar and Tsarina looked on. Rasputin declared that Anna would eventually recover but be crippled. He turned out to be correct. After her recovery, Viroubova became even more fervent in her supporter of Rasputin. Alexandra, in turn, did her best to encourage Nicholas II to believe in Rasputin's wisdom, that he knew what was best for Russia and for autocracy. In one letter, the Tsarina urged the Tsar to "harken unto our Friend, believe Him, He has your interest and Russians at heart … His words are not lightly spoken – and the gravity of having not only His prayers, but His advice – is great."

Besides Rasputin's ability to help the critically ill Viroubova and the young Alexei, the Tsarina was also drawn to him because he championed autocracy as the right type of government for Russia. Rasputin told Tsarina Alexandra that God would bless her and Nicholas if they continued to try to uphold autocracy. Alexandra explained Rasputin's beliefs to her husband in June 1915, noting that, "he spoke so much and beautifully about what a Russian Emperor is. Though other Sovereigns are anointed and crowned, only the Russian one has been a real Anointed [one] for the last three hundred years!"

The Tsarina was determined that her husband should pass the crown to her son intact, imploring him to do what was right, portraying herself as the champion of the Tsar and Tsarevich, saying that, "I am but a woman fighting for her Master & Child, her two dearest ones on earth…"

In the meantime, Russia continued to be convulsed in war. The death rates were staggering. A shortage of supplies and ammunition greatly hindered the Russian war effort. Russian anger towards Germany was at an all-time high. Since the beginning of the war, a wave of anti-German sentiment had enveloped Russia. In response to this, the capital had been re-named 'Petrograd' to make it sound less Germanic than 'St. Petersburg.' But as Russia's losses mounted, anti-German sentiments grew shriller. The Tsarina, born a princess of Hesse, was increasingly seen as 'the German' and a traitor to Russia. The accusation had no merit; Alexandra herself had admitted to the British Ambassador to Russia, Sir George Buchanan, she had "broken all the ties that connected her with Germany." The Tsarina's brother-in-law, Sandro, vouched for Alexandra's Russian sympathies, stating that, "I knew her mistakes. I loathed Rasputin. I wished Alix would not take her synthetic palace-born picture of a Russian peasant for a reality, but I must admit that she was far above all her contemporaries in fervent Russian patriotism."

The Tsarina's unpopularity was such that there was talk of plots to oust her and have her locked up in a convent, plots which Alexandra was aware of. As she continued in her unswerving support of Rasputin, what little popularity Tsarina Alexandra had plummeted. When Sandro, in desperation, tried to "shake Nicky by the shoulder and ask him to wake up," he was met with anger. Upon discussing the political life in the Russian capital, Sandro was shocked by the Tsar's response. "Mistrust and coldness appeared in his eyes," recalled Sandro, "an expression never before seen by me during our forty-one years of friendship."

Half-jokingly, Sandro said to his beleaguered brother-in-law: "You do not seem to trust your friends any more, Nicky."

"I believe no one, but my wife," came the cold but frank reply.

By 1916, instability wracked Russia. A.A. Mossolov admitted that, "intrigues of every sort were being hatched in all directions, shooting up like poisonous fungi." Sir George Buchanan wrote that "the conduct of the war was venting itself in attacks on the Emperor and Empress." The Tsar's cousin, Grand Duchess Marie, noted how, "the Empress devoted herself completely to the care of the wounded; the Emperor continually visited the front." Yet this did not matter. "Their lack of popularity increased, while Rasputin's popularity was mounting and the tides of gossip about him spread farther, day by day." As for Tsarina Alexandra, Grand Duchess Marie recalled that: "On all hands, the Empress was criticized violently, and continually accused, quite unfairly, of desiring a separate peace."

Among the Romanov family, concerns over Rasputin's influence also grew. Efforts to detach Rasputin from the orbit of Nicholas and Alexandra failed. The Tsarina's own sister, Grand Duchess Elisabeth, warned her about the *staretz*, telling the Tsarina bluntly: "Remember the fate of Louis XVI and Marie Antoinette." Alexandra took no heed. Dowager Empress Marie tried to convince her son to be rid of Rasputin, but to no avail. She decried what was happening, blaming Tsarina Alexandra, saying that, "this is not Nicky, not him … it is all her." Of Rasputin, the Grand Duchess Marie admitted that she, her brother, Grand Duke Dmitri, and their father, Grand Duke Paul (an uncle of Tsar Nicholas), "simply despised him." Another Grand Duchess Marie, the aunt of the Tsar, warned Mikhail Rodzianko ominously of the Tsarina that, "she was driving the country to destruction; that she was the cause of the danger which threatened the Emperor…." Drastic measures had to employed insisted the incensed Grand Duchess. A shocked Rodzianko could not believe his ears when he heard the Tsar's aunt demand that the Tsarina "must be annihilated."

A.A. Mossolov summed up the crisis surrounding Rasputin: "The Press began to be full of references to Rasputin as a sinister adventurer and an indescribable curse to the country. It was continually being said that Rasputin controlled all the important appointments in the Orthodox Church; it was whispered that he had the ear of the Empress."

Tsarina Alexandra ignored all the clamor and criticisms. To her, Rasputin continued to be "almost a saint, endowed with the mysterious power of relieving and curing the little Tsarevitch whose health was a constant and continual anxiety, and obstinately she refused to listen to the many warnings given her." Such was the conclusion of Meriel Buchanan. As daughter of Sir George Buchanan, British ambassador to Russia from 1910-17, Meriel, who lived in the capital, saw first-hand, historic events enveloping Russia and the imperial family.

The Tsarina earned the enmity of many who blamed her for the increasing instability in the government thanks to her insistence on who should hold significant ministerial positions, mostly based on Rasputin's advice. She was unstinting in her opinions to Nicholas II about who should stay and who should go in his government. Alexandra's championing of Alexander Protopopov as Minister of the Interior in 1916 with Rasputin's support, was greeted with incredulity. Protopopov was seen as incompetent whose sanity was questioned. This appointment had a direct negative effect on Tsarina Alexandra. According to the Tsar's cousin, Grand Duchess Marie, "it was about this time that I first heard people speaking of the Emperor and Empress with open animosity and contempt. The word 'revolution' was uttered more openly and more often; soon it could be heard everywhere. The war seemed to recede in the background. All attention was riveted on interior events. Rasputin, Rasputin, Rasputin – it was like a refrain; his mistakes, his shocking personal conduct, his mysterious power. This power was tremendous; it was like dusk, enveloping all our world, eclipsing the sun. How could so pitiful a wretch throw so vast a shadow? It was inexplicable, maddening, baffling, almost incredible."

In the meantime, the war continued unabated. For the average Russian private, "the war had been accompanied by the hope of a free and more happy life in Russia itself; and now that that hope had failed, defeatism, depression and demoralization were growing apace."

In Petrograd, government ministers came and went with rapidity, amounting to a kind of chaotic ministerial musical chairs. Competent ministers gave way to inconsequential and weak men who failed to help Russia. The chaos and seemingly nefarious influence of Rasputin prompted Alexander Trepov, the Prime Minister, to attempt to get Rasputin out of the way once and for all by bribing him to leave permanently for Siberia and stay out of political affairs. This failed. Rasputin reported the incident to the Tsarina. Trepov became a marked man, destined for dismissal. Rasputin, in turn, enhanced his reputation in the eyes of Tsarina Alexandra, for he proved to be an "incorruptible man of the people."

Throughout all the chaos the Tsarina remained resolute. She knew she was loathed. But this did not deter her. The Tsarina urged Nicholas II to listen to Rasputin's advice and not Trepov, telling him: "He [Rasputin] entreats you to be firm, to be the Master and not always to give in to Trepov … Remember why I am disliked – shows it right to be firm and feared and you be the same, you a man – only believe more in our Friend. He lives for you and Russia." Tsarina Alexandra's iron will was tempered with pleadings to her husband to think of their only son and heir: "we must give a strong country to Baby, and dare not be weak for his sake, else he will have a yet harder reign … Let our legacy be a lighter one for Alexei. He has a strong will and mind of his own, don't let things slip through your fingers and make him have to build up all again."

Keeping the throne intact for Alexei to inherit was of great importance to the Tsarina, but it was her son's health, above all, which was uppermost in her mind. Rasputin's presence had to be maintained if, for the sole reason of keeping Alexei alive, who, by this stage, had suffered much. The hemophilia attacks had taken a toll on the Tsarevich. The delicate state of Alexei's health was evident to those who came into contact with him. Princess Paley, a great-aunt to the heir, was one such individual. Upon meeting Alexei in the autumn of 1916, Princess Paley noted that, "the Tsarevitch, with his refined and charming countenance, struck me by his look of fragility. The thinness of his neck distracted me. One could have taken it with two fingers." And yet, Alexei maintained his good spirits as much as he could. During this visit with Princess Paley and her son, the Princess noted that, "the dear little Tsarevitch seemed to be amusing himself enormously. His parents had all the difficulty in the world to get him away…"

Tragically for Alexei and his mother, Rasputin's seeming ability to help the heir with his hemophilia attacks had little or no bearing on the decision of individuals such as Trepov to eliminate him from the scene. Incalculable damage had already been wreaked on the monarchy due to Rasputin's presence and in order to help the dynasty and Russia, the *staretz* had to go. Trepov's failed last ditch attempt at banishing Rasputin led to the conclusion from certain individuals that the only way to eliminate Rasputin was to pursue the most drastic measure: someone had to kill him. The plan came from the highest echelons of society with close connections to the Tsar. Two individuals involved in the plot included Prince Felix Yussopov, the eccentric twenty-nine-year-old scion of Russia's wealthiest family and married to Princess Irina, niece of Nicholas II; the other was twenty-five-year-old Grand Duke Dmitri, once thought to be a possible husband for Nicholas and Alexandra's eldest daughter, Grand Duchess Olga.

Yussopov and Dmitri hatched a plan to rid Russia once and for all of the hated Rasputin. Vladimir Purishkevich a member of the Duma, supported them. When Purishkevich spoke at length with Yussopov about what to do about the notorious *staretz,* Yussopov gave his unflinching reply: "Remove Rasputin."

Rasputin was no stranger to Yussopov, who had met him several times and spoke to him at length. Rasputin even had once admitted to Yussopov that when it came to those who criticized him, "I don't care what a lot of nincompoops write and say, I scorn them, they're only harming themselves."

Yusspov himself felt the un-explicable strength of Rasputin's hypnotic abilities. When Rasputin fixed his steely gaze upon him, Felix recalled how, "I felt as if some active energy were pouring heat, like a warm current, into my whole being. I fell into a torpor, and my body grew numb; I tried to speak, but my tongue no longer obeyed me and I gradually slipped into a drowsy state, as though a powerful narcotic had been administered to me."

In December 1916, Rasputin accepted an invitation from Yussopov to visit him in his magnificent palace on the Moika River in the Russian capital. The plot to annihilate Rasputin was put into action. What then transpired was the stuff of novels. Yussopov entertained the Rasputin while Grand Duke Dmitri and Purishkevich were in another room, nervously waiting.

The plot to assassinate Rasputin took place in the dead of night. Yussopov plied Rasputin with poisoned cake and madeira but to his astonishment, the *staretz* did not succumb to the poison. At one point, Rasputin stared at Yussopov with a spiteful look and said eerily: "Now, see, you're wasting your time, you can't do anything to me."

Felix Yussopov later wrote that, "I had the feeling that he knew why I had brought him to my house, and what I had set out to do. We seemed to be engaged in a strange and terrible struggle."

Yussopov left a groggy Rasputin on his own in order to speak to Purishkevich and Dmitri. Purishkevich declared that Rasputin had to be finished off. Yussopov took a revolver belonging to Dmitri and returned to the basement where Rasputin was, shooting him in the heart. Dmitri and Purishkevich rushed to Yussopov's side and examined the seemingly lifeless body of Rasputin.

Yussopov recalled how, "our hearts were full of hope for we were convinced that what had just taken place would save Russia and the dynasty from ruin and dishonor."

Not long after he shot Rasputin, Yussopov returned on his own to the basement and shook the corpse. To Yussopov's astonishment, Rasputin was alive, foaming at the mouth. He struggled to his feet and rushed toward Yussopov. Rasputin had done the seemingly impossible; he returned from the dead. Yussopov, who was soon joined by Purishkevich ran after Rasputin who had made his way outside. Incredulously, Purishkevich heard a staggering Rasputin mutter, "Felix, Felix. I'll tell it all to the Czarina."

An incredulous Purishkevich took out his revolver and shot at Rasputin, felling him. When

Felix, wrought with fear and emotion, encountered Rasputin's corpse in the snow, he began to beat it hysterically then fainted.

Purishkevich, Grand Duke Dmitri, and another accomplice helped dispose of Rasputin's body. They threw it into the nearby Moika canal. The battered body was soon fished out of the icy water.

Tsarina Alexandra had heard from Protopopov about Rasputin's disappearance. She hoped Rasputin was not dead but in hiding. "I cannot & *won't* believe it," insisted Alexandra. The French Ambassador to Russia, Maurice Paléologue, noted how, "the Empress is stricken with grief. She has begged the Emperor, who is at Mohilev [*Stavka*] to return to her at once."

As for Nicholas II, he took the news of Rasputin's assassination far better than his wife. According to the Tsar's aide, "I did not once observe signs of sorrow in His Majesty, but rather gathered the impression that he experienced a sense of relief."

When the Tsarina finally accepted the fact that Rasputin was dead, she cried for the man who had helped her son through his torturous ordeals.

She also ordered that Rasputin's body be buried in a chapel in Tsarskoe Selo. To the Tsarina, Rasputin had become a martyr.

Grand Duchess Marie, Dmitri's sister, wondered what the Tsarina's thoughts could have been upon learning of Rasputin's assassination. Marie, who was hostile toward Alexandra, nevertheless conceded that, "my heart perceived her torture."

As far as the Tsar was concerned, Rasputin's assassination was a crime that demanded punishment. Nicholas II banished Grand Duke Dmitri to the front in Persia and as for Prince Felix Yussopov, the Tsar banished him to one of his numerous estates in Russia.

When Yussopov's father-in-law, the very same Sandro who was also the Tsar's brother-in-law, tried to argue in defense of Felix and Dmitri, as "misguided patriots," Nicholas II replied, "a very nice speech, Sandro." Then the Tsar added: "Are you aware, however, that nobody has the right to kill, be it a grand duke or peasant?"

Other Romanov family members also tried to help Felix and Dmitri. They wrote collectively, a letter to the Tsar begging him to be lenient. The letter resulted in an open breach between Nicholas and Alexandra and their Romanov relations. A.A. Mossolov concluded that this incident made things clear to Nicholas, for "the Tsar saw the whole of the Romanovs ranged against himself and his wife."

Grand Duchess Marie sought to explain Dmitri's actions in the assassination of Rasputin: "Forgetting himself, he had stepped between the people and the imperial couple; he had sought to save his sovereigns in spite of themselves. Would they ever be able to realize that?"

The Tsar and Tsarina saw Rasputin's killing not as some kind of patriotic act, ridding them of a nefarious individual. Instead, the imperial couple saw the act as plain murder. The Tsar's reply to the collective letter written by the Romanovs asking that he pardon Grand Duke Dmitri made this clear: "I do not permit anyone to give me advice. Murder is murder. Moreover I know that several among those who have signed this letter have not got a clean conscience either." On the margin of the letter, an angry Nicholas wrote, emphatically, "Nobody has a right of assassination!"

The one most affected by the assassination of Rasputin was undoubtedly the Tsarina Alexandra. Of the Tsarina, Sophie Buxhoeveden wrote that, "she felt sad and tired." Moreover, "she had pinned all her faith on him as the saviour of her child. With Rasputin at hand she had been at rest about her boy, whose days she now felt were numbered." For Rasputin had prophesied to the Tsarina and the Tsar: "If I die or you desert me, you will lose your son and your crown within six months."

With Rasputin now dead, would the ominous warnings he had given the Tsarina come frighteningly to fruition?

Chapter 7.   Revolution (1917)

For Tsarina Alexandra, Rasputin's assassination was terrifying to contemplate. The very existence of her only son, Alexei, had depended upon Rasputin's ability to help him, and now he was dead. As far as the rest of Russia was concerned, Rasputin's death ushered in an uncertain era in the country's chaotic landscape. To the peasants, Rasputin had been one of them and so, according to Maurice Paléolgoue, "their explanation of the crime is therefore a simple one: the enemies of the people killed the staretz because he pleaded the people's cause before the Tsar." Others were much more jubilant. Upon learning of the deed done on Rasputin by Prince Felix Yussopov and Grand Duke Dmitri, people knelt before the palaces of Felix and Dmitri in gratitude. Services of thanksgiving were held in churches. Audiences in theaters sung the national anthem repeatedly. Yussopov recalled how, "we were toasted in regimental messes; factory workers gave cheers in our honor. Letters from all parts of Russia brought us thanks and blessings." But not surprisingly, Rasputin's partisans "did not forget us either; they covered us with abuse and uttered dire threats."

The disappearance of Rasputin from the scene did not have the desired effect that Prince Felix Yussopov, Grand Duke Dmitri, and Vladimir Purishkevich had hoped. The high price the war exacted out of Russia had sapped the people's hope. By the time of Rasputin's assassination, the Romanov dynasty had totally lost the people's respect and confidence. Bread was scarce. Violence increased. Rioting broke out. Petrograd was a powder keg, a volcano waiting to erupt. Revolution was in the air.

The Tsar found himself in a difficult situation. He was torn by two dominant sentiments. As Pierre Gilliard put it, "one of them was his love for his country and the other his absolute determination to continue the war to the bitter end." Prince Felix Yussopov concluded that, "toward the end of his reign, Nicolas II was crushed by anxiety and disheartened by his political misadventures. He was a confirmed fatalist, and convinced that it was useless to struggle against destiny."

Alexander Trepov was replaced from his position as Prime Minister not long after Rasputin's assassination. In Maurice Paléologue's eyes, Trepov's departure was a disaster, for "I fear that in this blunt and faithful servant the monarchy of the tsars is also losing its last pillar and its last safeguard." Trepov was replaced by Prince Nikolai Golitsyn, who, according to Sandro, "understood nothing, knew nothing." Together with Protopopov as Interior Minister, both "presented a pair extraordinarily fit for the last act of the Death of a Nation."

In January 1917, Tsar Nicholas was bluntly told by a close friend, Admiral Nilov, that the Tsarina should be sent away; it was the only thing that could save the dynasty and Russia. Nilov had admired Tsarina Alexandra, but he saw that she was widely seen as the cause of so much trouble. The Tsar rebuked Nilov.

"The Empress is a foreigner," said Nicholas II. "She has no one to protect her but myself. I shall never abandon her, under any circumstances. In any case, all the charges made against her are false. Wicked lies are being told about her. But I shall know how to make her respected!"

The Tsar's mother, the Dowager Empress Marie Feodorovna, living far from the capital in Kiev, wrote to her son in these anxious days, telling him, "I can only pray to God for you, that He support you and inspire you to do all you can for the good of our dear Russia."

Tsar Nicholas II had tried to rule Russia as best as he could. He confided as such to Mikhail Rodzianko in January 1917 when the Tsar, pressing his head in his hands, admitted with a heavy heart: "Is it possible that for twenty-two years I tried to work for the best, and that for twenty-two years it was all a mistake?"

Nicholas II had, according to Sir George Buchanan, who knew him, possessed "many gifts that would have fitted him to play the part of a constitutional Sovereign – a quick intelligence, a cultivated mind, method and industry in his work, and an extraordinary natural charm that attracted all who came near him." Count Paul Benckendorff, a close associate of Nicholas II, was of a similar mind when he noted of the Tsar that: "He was very intelligent, understood things at once, and was very quick, but he did not know how to reconcile his decisions with the fundamental political principles which he entirely lacked." What good qualities the Tsar had were not enough to stem the revolutionary tide that brought down the Romanov dynasty.

The Tsar continued to divide his time between *Stavka* and Tsarskoe Selo. Despite the disheartening events, Nicholas II was still hopeful that when it came to his army, they would come through. According to Pierre Gilliard, the Tsar, "was certain that his army would be ready in the spring in that great offensive of the Allies which would deal Germany her death-blow and thus save Russia: a few weeks more and victory would be his."

But before the warmth of spring could arrive, Russia had to endure winter with its freezing temperatures and snow storms. The bitter winter meant trouble for the army and people of the capital, for food supplies were hard to come by, leaving them in dire straits. Famine threatened. In Petrograd, Felix Yusspov wrote that life "grew daily more depressing." By the end of February 1917, there was hardly any food to be found in Petrograd. Strikes and insurrection were the order of the day. Rioting broke out. Crowds shouting their anger and gun shots piercing the air were common. Authorities were losing control of the capital. Then, a mutiny broke out in the garrison of Petrograd. This frightening turn of events meant that over 150,000 soldiers were in outright rebellion. This spelt danger. Without the loyalty of the troops, the dynasty was in deep danger. The mutiny of the Pavlovsky Regiment was especially symbolic. On Sunday, February 26, a sunny warm day that gave a hint of spring, 1,500 men from the Pavlovsky barracks fired on the police. The mutinous actions electrified Petrograd. It was, according to one contemporary observer, a "breach in the stronghold of Czarism."

At *Stavka* in Moghilev, Nicholas II was assailed with anxiety during these trying times, recording in his diary: "It's a revolting sensation to be so far away to receive only scraps of bad news!"

On that final Sunday in February, Count Paul Benckendorff, described the state of siege that had gripped the capital, stating that, "the revolution, which for some days had raged in St. Petersburg, spread through the whole city; the troops, reserve battalions, ill-recruited and ill-led, had nearly all of them gone over to the side of the revolution, and towards evening only a few battalions remained faithful to the Emperor and to their oath. These occupied the Winter Palace and the Admiralty. The revolutionaries were victorious in the town."

It now became imperative to try and save the Tsarina and her children at the Alexander Palace. Nicholas II ordered that a train should be made ready for his wife and children. He prepared to return to Tsarskoe Selo. Meanwhile, the loyal soldiers holding the Winter Palace could not offer much help. They were "dying of hunger," according to General Khabalov, the commander of the military district of the capital in his frantic phone call to Count Benckendorff at Tsarskoe Selo, overseeing the safety of the Tsarina and her children. "The panic which was plain in all his words," Benckendorff noted, "proved to me that there was no more hope and that resistance could only last a few more hours."

At Tsarskoe Selo, Tsarina Alexandra was under no illusions as to the dangerous state of affairs. Referring to her daughters, the Tsarina said to Lili Dehn, "I don't want the girls to know anything until it is impossible to keep the truth from them…" The Tsarina busied herself trying to be solicitous to the faithful retainers who remained by her family's side, such as Lili Dehn, Anna Viroubova, Sophie Buxhoeveden, and Pierre Gilliard. Besides her anxieties for those around her and for her suffering subjects, Tsarina Alexandra was also nursing her children who, according to Dehn, were "lying desperately ill" with the measles. The Tsarevich Alexei at one point was particularly hot to the touch, with a fever hovering dangerously at 104 degrees Fahrenheit. In Dehn's words, the imperial children, so desperately ill, looked "almost like corpses." The Alexander Palace was "terror-stricken, and outside brooded the dread spectre of Revolution!"

During these harrowing days, in her role as mother, Tsarina Alexandra never faltered. In delicate health herself, the Tsarina never failed to climb the stairs to visit her sick children, despite the effort and toll it took on her. "This sounds a trivial incident," noted Lili Dehn, "but it entailed a great deal of suffering on the Empress, who was overtired and overstrung. Her heart, always affected, now became much worse, owing to her having to go up and down stairs so often, but she insisted upon seeing her children, and she used to go up the staircase at times almost on the verge of fainting."

All this took place without the presence of Tsar Nicholas II at Tsarskoe Selo. The lack of news from her husband sent Alexandra into spasms of worry. According to Sophie Buxhoevden who was with her, the Tsarina "could scarcely master her anxiety." More alarming news came when those in the Alexander Palace learned that the Tsarskoe Selo garrison had mutinied. Prisoners were let loose and looted liquor shops. "They intended to seize the Empress and the heir," according to Buxhoeveden, "and take them to the Revolutionary Headquarters Staff at Petrograd." The Tsarina tried to calm her sick children, telling them that all the indiscriminate gun shots they heard were due merely to maneuvers going on.

Tsarina Alexandra did not want blood shed on her account. In the dark of night, with the reflection of the white snow acting as a faint light, Tsarina Alexandra spoke to the soldiers guarding the Alexander Palace and told hem how she trusted fully in their fidelity to the Tsar and "how well she knew that if need arose they would defend the heir, but that she hoped that no blood need be shed. The scene," wrote Buxhoevden for posterity, "was unforgettable."

In the palace, the situation was increasingly strained. Revolutionaries cut off the water supply and electricity. Tsarina Alexandra and Sophie Buxhoeveden found themselves walking down "the vast dark halls" of the palace, their shoes echoing "uncannily in the empty rooms." As the situation around her grew more frightening, Tsarina Alexandra, despite her ill health, never stopped thinking of those around her. She brought pillows and blankets from her own room to give to her retainers for their use.

For Tsarina Alexandra, a terrible blow was dealt her when her beloved Garde Equipage deserted her and the Alexander Palace when their Commander-in-Chief, the Grand Duke Kyril, sent for them. In a broken, despairing voice, Tsarina Alexandra muttered to Lili Dehn: "My sailors – my *own* sailors – I can't believe it."

Meanwhile, the Tsar was desperate to return to Tsarskoe Selo. When the Tsarina had been informed that the Tsar was on his way back, she told Count Benckendorff that she would not leave with the children to flee owing to the serious ill state of their health. She would await Nicholas II's arrival. The Tsar's train, however, was stopped at Pskov. Upon learning that Petrograd was in revolt with mobs killing at random and with Moscow suffering the same fate, Mikhail Rodzianko advised that the Tsar should abdicate. "Otherwise anarchy would get the upper hand," noted General Loukhomsky, who had been Quartermaster-General at Russian General Headquarters, "and this would mean a separate peace with Germany. Rodzianko stated further that the abdication of the Emperor was the only way to put an end to the wholesale murders of officials true to their oath of allegiance [to the Tsar]." Of that moment, Loukhomsky wrote, "the situation was difficult in the extreme." Several generals advised Nicholas II that abdication was the only answer. Nikolasha telegraphed the Tsar, saying, "I must on my knees ask Your Imperial Majesty to save Russia and your heir ... Making a sign of the cross, transfer your heritage to him."

The Tsar let it be known that whatever it was the Duma wanted from him, he would concede in order to restore peace to the country. Rodzianko replied by telegraph that it was "too late." In order to avoid civil war, the Tsar took the momentous step of choosing to abdicate. It was a difficult choice to make, not so much because Nicholas II craved power, but that he did not want to renege on his coronation oath. Maurice Paléologue summed it up when he said of Nicholas II, that he "does not enjoy the exercise of power. If he jealously upholds his autocratic prerogatives, it is solely on mystical grounds. He never forgets that he has received his power from God Himself, and is always reminding himself that he will have to account for it in the valley of Josaphat."

At this significant moment when his reign was in the balance, Nicholas II's thoughts were on his beloved son. The Tsar summoned one of the Tsarevich's doctors and said, "Tell me frankly, Sergius Petrovitch. Is Alexis's malady incurable?"

Fully aware of the gravity of his reply, Dr. Feodorov said in full honesty: "Science teaches us, sire, that it is an incurable disease. Yet those who are afflicted with it sometimes reach an advanced old age. Still, Alexis Nicolaïvitch is at the mercy of an accident."

The Tsar, overcome with the news, murmured sadly: "That's just what the Czarina told me. Well, if that is the case and Alexis can never serve his county as I should like him to, we have the right to keep him ourselves."

A similar theme played out when the Tsar, who had aged and was gaunt and grayer, spoke of Alexei, to a Duma member, Alexander Guchkov, who had traveled to Pskov. When Guchkov told the Tsar and he and his family would likely have to leave Russia and live abroad, Nicholas asked, "shall I be able to take the Tsarevich with me?" If Alexei were the new sovereign, the answer was no, said Guchkov. Nicholas then replied that "although he was ready to make every sacrifice for the welfare of the Fatherland, it was more than he could do to part with his son, and that he would never consent to such a thing."

The Tsar had said directly to Gruchkov in a quiet tone, "I hope you will understand the feelings of a father."

Guchkov, surprised by the move, said to the Tsar: "But we had counted on the figure of the little Alexis Nikolaevich as having a softening effect on the transfer of power." There was something to be said in Guchkov's thinking, for "an innocent boy Emperor would have attracted sympathy, rallied loyalists, signaled continuity and disarmed those who paraded the crimes of the Romanovs as justification for bringing down the monarchist state."

Nothing would dissuade the Tsar from being separated from his beloved son. Nicholas II took the unprecedented step of abdicating for himself and Alexei on March 2, 1917, declaring that the throne should pass to his brother, Grand Duke Michael. In this supremely significant moment in Russian history, Tsar Nicholas II, according to one historian, "was master of the situation. Here was a part to play which was entirely in keeping with the best and highest in his character … he was returning to the role …. of the good loser, the willing accepter of defeat."

The abdication text was a moving document that spoke of the troubles besetting Russia and of the Tsar's desire to do what was best for his country. "The destiny of Russia," the momentous document stated, "the honour of our heroic army, the good of the people, the whole future of our dear country demand that whatever it cost, the war should be brought to a victorious end. In these decisive days in the life of Russia, we have thought it a duty of conscience to facilitate for our people a close union and consolidation of all national forces for the speedy attainment of victory; and, in agreement with the Imperial Duma, we have thought it good to abdicate from the throne of the Russian State, and to lay down the supreme power." Then in a poignant indication of what the sickly Alexei meant to his father, the Tsar continued: "Not wishing to part with our dear son, we hand over our inheritance to our brother, Grand Duke Michael … May the Lord God help Russia!"

Numerous individuals were surprised by the substitution of Michael for Alexei in the instrument of abdication. According to Nicolas de Basily, who drafted the original abdication document, "the immediate accession of the Tsarevitch was the only means of stopping the revolution in its career … If the Tsarevitch had been proclaimed, no one would have had the authority to make him abdicate."

Whether it was Alexei or Michael who was to be the next monarch, the deed was done, Nicholas II had ceded the throne, "an event of gigantic significance." Alexander Guchkov took note of the atmosphere surrounding the Tsar at this grave moment in Russian history. Guchkov "noticed how those around him who were the

Emperor's own men, showed a complete indifference to his fate." Later that night, the former Tsar confided in his diary: "All around, treachery, cowardice and deceit."

Numerous individuals could not fathom that the Tsar had abdicated. Count Benckendorff could not believe how Nicholas II "had so quickly consented to abdicate. The part played by the Generals and the Staff seemed to us like treason."

The former Tsar's cousin, Grand Duchess Marie, found that, "the decision of the Emperor to abdicate for the Tsarevich caught us unawares. No one had expected him to take that step."

The French Ambassador, Paléologue, ever careful to record the historic events he was living through in Petrograd, noted that Grand Duke Michael's accession to the throne was met with derision and "aroused the fury of the *Soviet*: 'No more Romanovs!'"

Two days after the Tsar's abdication, Paléologue wrote of the "very dismal" weather in Petrograd. Heavy snow fell in "dense flakes" leaving the Ambassador to conclude that "the gloom of the landscape and the enmity of nature harmonize only too well with the sinister course events are taking."

At the Alexander Palace, Grand Duke Paul, the former Tsar's uncle, had the unenviable task of breaking the tragic news to Alexandra. The Grand Duke, his heart palpitating like mad, was at first unable to utter a word to the former Tsarina, dressed in her hospital nurse's uniform. He was struck by "her calm and the serenity of her gaze."

Grand Duke Paul said to Alexandra that Nicholas had "signed his abdication for himself and for Alexis."

With tears falling down her cheeks, Alexandra replied, "if Nicky has done that, it is because he had to do so. I have faith in the Divine Mercy. God will not abandon us." She then continued, saying, "I am no longer Empress but I remain a Sister of Charity ... I shall look after my children and my hospital."

Lili Dehn was the first person to see Alexandra after the painful audience with Grand Duke Paul. "Her face was distorted with agony," recalled Dehn, "her eyes were full of tears."

Leaning on a writing table, the former Tsarina took Lili's hands in hers and said in a broken voice: "*Abdiqué!*"

Alexandra was also overcome with emotion when the thought came to her that her husband had been alone in this time of trial. And then Alexandra cried in fear about Alexei to Lili, saying: "Now *he'll* be taken from me." The former Tsarina became a nervous wreck, trembling "at the mere sound of a voice … One idea obsessed her," noted Dehn, "someone might come at any moment to take away her son!"

Alexei, the longed-for heir, the child of his mother's many tears, had to be told of the news of the abdication. Alexandra, her mother's heart pained by the onerous task, asked Pierre Gilliard to break the news to the twelve-year-old.

"You know your father does not want to be Czar any more, Alexis Nicolaëvitch," said Gilliard.

Astonished, Alexei tried to read Gilliard's face for clues as to what had occurred. "What! Why?" said the bewildered child.

"He is very tired and has had a lot of trouble lately."

"Oh yes! Mother told me they stopped his train when he wanted to come here. But won't Papa be Czar again afterwards?"

Gilliard said that Nicholas II had abdicated in favor of Alexei's uncle, the Grand Duke Michael, who refused the throne.

"But who's going to be Czar, then?" said Alexei in consternation, his face red.

"I don't know. Perhaps nobody now …"

Gilliard noted that for Alexei, that there was "not a word about himself. Not a single allusion to his rights as the Heir."

An anxious Alexei peppered his mother with questions, saying, "Shall I never go to G.H.Q. [*Stavka*] again with Papa?"

"No, my darling – never again," came Alexandra's reply.

"Shan't I see my regiments and my soldiers?"

"No … I fear not."

"Oh dear! And the yacht, and all my friends on board – shall we never go yachting any more?" At this point the boy was nearly in tears.

"No … we shall never see the Standart … It does not belong to us now."

The family was now at the mercy of others. The Tsar had abdicated for himself and his sickly heir, obliterating the Romanov dynasty's three-hundred-year rule. With the end of the Romanovs in power, what kind of fate awaited Nicholas and Alexandra?

Chapter 8.   Captivity (1917-1918)

Nicholas's return to Tsarskoe Selo six days after his abdication, was greeted with relief by his family. In the evening of his arrival, Nicholas and Alexandra dined together. Alone together at last, Nicholas let out a torrent of emotions and "wept bitterly." Alexandra had difficulty consoling her husband, assuring him that "the husband and father was of more value in her eyes than the Emperor whose throne she had shared."

No longer Tsar of Russia, the former Nicholas II had become simply 'Citizen Romanov.' And as the former Tsarina stated to Grand Duke Paul, she would be content merely to be a nursing sister and mother watching over her children. The former Grand Duchesses: Olga, Tatiana, Marie, and Anastasia never wavered throughout the ensuing difficult months in their devotion to their parents and brother. And as for Alexei, whose health began to improve, he did not appear to notice much change around him at first, "except when he missed certain of his soldiers and his friends." In the eyes of Lili Dehn, "he was still a happy, light-hearted child."

As for Alexei's uncle, Michael, he found himself in a quandary: should he take up the mantle of Tsar or should he reject it. Michael listened to debates about how to proceed with the unexpected predicament he found himself in. In the end, not long after Nicholas II abdicated, Michael, too, forfeited the throne. The Minister of Justice in the newly formed Provisional Government, Alexander Kerensky, who was vehement that Michael not become the next Tsar, declared to him that, "you are the noblest of men!"

Kerensky became the jailer of the former Tsar and Tsarina who remained isolated with their family at the Alexander Palace, prisoners in their own home. For the next sixteen months, the family endured trials and tribulations. In the eyes of one contemporary, "the prisoners had to ascend a Calvary that grew harder and steeper with every day that passed."

No longer Tsarina of Russia, Alexandra could have let the bitter experiences of the past harden her and turn her into a vengeful woman, especially when she saw former loyal retainers desert her and her family. Instead, "from this time begins the real test of her character, which she was to pass through with growing courage to the end." Anna Viroubova, always a devoted friend to Alexandra, described the former Tsarina in admiring terms, recalling how "she lost none of her marvelous courage. She did not call upon the Ministers or the Allied Ambassadors to protect her or her children. With dignity unmoved, she witnessed day by day the cowardly desertion of men who for years had lived at Court and who had enjoyed the faith and friendship of the Imperial Family."

The elimination of Rasputin and the revolution that toppled the Tsar did nothing to improve Nicholas and Alexandra's situation. The former Tsarina was still derided as that 'German woman' who was a traitor to Russia. The Dowager Empress, aggrieved at the turn of events, was shocked at the callousness with which her family had been viewed as "Enemies of the Revolution and the Russian people." She told Sandro that, "my unfortunate Nicky may have made some mistakes, but to say that he is an enemy of his people – Ah, never, never…"

Life at Tsarskoe Selo for the former Tsar and his family changed dramatically from that of being a home to that of being a prison. They were constantly watched and subjected to humiliations. Impertinent, crude soldiers roamed at will, shouting: "Where is the Heir?" "Show us the Heir?" The family endured with dignity rudeness and humiliations thrown at them by the soldiers assigned to watch over them. Count Benckendorff, who stayed on with the family at Tsarskoe Selo, found that "the soldiers – with rare exceptions – were so rude that it was impossible to speak to them."

For a month, Nicholas and Alexandra were separated by their captors and only spoke to each other at meals. Neither complained of the constraints imposed on them by Kerensky, including his decision to eject Anna Viroubova and Lili Dehn from the Alexander Palace. Anna, ill with the measles, was locked away in the Fortress of Saints Peter and Paul where she languished for five months. In that same month, a scene played out that cut at the heart of Nicholas's aunt-by-marriage, Princess Paley, whose husband, Grand Duke Paul, had broken the news to Alexandra of the Tsar's abdication. While watching Nicholas break the ice in the park at Tsarskoe Selo, Princess Paley joined a small crowd to watch him. Pressing her cheeks against the barrier's bars, Princess Paley heard the soldiers surrounding Nicholas taunt him mercilessly, saying: "Well, well, Nicolouchka (Little Nicholas), so you are breaking the ice now, are you? Perhaps you've drunk enough of our blood? ... And in summer, when there's no more ice – what'll you do then, *Gloubchik nach* (our darling)? Perhaps you'll throw a little sand on the walks with a little shovel?"

Nicholas did not miss a word of the painful insults the soldiers hurled at him. Nevertheless, Nicholas remained dignified in his silence. The incident shook Princess Paley. "There was something satanic in their laughter," she wrote of what she had witnessed. Nicholas stopped what he was doing and "took a long, sad look at them." He turned to Princess Paley with a "mournful gaze" in which the Princess read in "his dear eyes a misery so deep, a hopeless resignation so great" that hot bitter tears welled in her eyes.

During Nicholas and Alexandra's captivity at Tsarskoe Selo, Alexander Kerensky in his capacity as their jailor came to know the couple. In April, Kerensky spoke at some length to the former Tsarina whom he discovered to be frank. She said that she and the former Tsar were "the most united of couples, whose whole joy and pleasure was in their family life, and that they had no secrets from each other: that they discussed everything..." Kerensky "was struck by the clarity, the energy and the frankness of her words." Kerensky admitted to the former Tsar that, "your wife does not lie." Kerensky concluded that Alexandra had not been a German spy but was loyal to Russia.

During their captivity at Tsarskoe Selo, the former Tsarevich and his younger sisters were allowed to continue with their lessons. Nicholas, his children, and some of the retainers were also allowed to cut wood for winter and to dig and tend to a small kitchen garden. There were some moments of peace for the family; but inevitably they were subjected to the rude and insolent behavior of the soldiers. In one stance, seeing

Alexei playing with a small toy gun, the soldiers snatched it away from the boy. And yet through their trials, the family bore everything with patience. Instead of meeting their hardships and humiliations with complaints, they met them with disciplined dignity. The soldiers eventually "learned that they were guarding a family who were quiet, unprovocative, unfailingly polite to one another and to them, and whose occasional sadness bore the stamp of a dignity their jailers could never emulate and were reluctantly compelled to admire."

Religion provided an enduring comfort and was the source of strength for Nicholas, Alexandra, and their children throughout their captivity. Religious services were periodically allowed and this, the family eagerly partook in. In June 1917, Alexandra had written to Lili Dehn, telling her that: "One can find in everything something good and useful – whatever sufferings we go through - let it be. He will give us force and patience and will not leave us. He is merciful. It is only necessary to bow to His wish without murmur and await – there on the other side He is preparing to all who love Him undescribable joy." On Alexei's fourteenth birthday in July 1917, his mother wrote to Lili of her happiness that it was possible for her to have an icon of the Blessed Mother "at this day dear to me."

On the day of Alexei's birthday, Divine Liturgy had been conducted and a procession of the clergy with the venerated icon of Our Lady of Znamenie took place. Count Benckendorff, who participated, noted that "the ceremony was as poignant as could be: all were in tears." Even the soldiers "themselves seemed touched, and approached the holy Ikon to kiss it." To Benckendorff, it was as if "the past were taking leave, never to come back."

Benckendorrff was overcome with emotion when it came to Alexei. The Count had accepted an invitation, along with other faithful retainers, from Alexei to watch a film in his room. Count Benckendorff saw that Alexei "enjoyed acting as host, and received us with a childish animation which was charming to see." Benckendorff was moved by the potential future Alexei could offer, noting that of the former Tsarevich: "He is very intelligent, has a great deal of character and an excellent heart. If his disease could be mastered, and should God grant him life, he should one day play a part in the restoration of our poor country.

He is the representative of the legitimate principle; his character has been formed by the misfortunes of his parents and of his childhood. May God protect him and save him and all his family from the claws of the fanatics in which they are at present!"

Such was the difficult life of the former imperial family at Tsarskoe Selo. Petrograd, meanwhile, continued to seethe. Prince Vladimir Paley, half-brother of Grand Duke Dmitri, confided in diary that the city "smells of blood. The city is unspeakably dirty. Chaotic crowds, disorder, anarchy. In one word – revolution."

The Petrograd Soviet were proving to be a menace to the Provisional Government. In April, Vladimir Lenin, the socialist firebrand who opposed the war and was the leader of the Bolsheviks had returned from exile to Russia, determined to take over the revolution. The war had continued under the Provisional Government, but the Germans hoped that Lenin's return would wreck the Russian war effort. Lenin, though, was forced to flee again in July.

As for the former imperial family, uncertainty continued to cloud their fate. Attempts to spirit them out of Russia and into exile in

England failed. "Time had been lost," recalled the former Tsar's brother-in-law, Sandro, "and the real masters of the situation, the heads of the St. Petersburg Soviet, insisted on a Siberian exile."

After being in captivity for nearly seventeen months, Nicholas and Alexandra and their children were ordered out of the Alexander Palace their home for many years. In August 1917, the family assembled in the main hall of the palace. "The soldiers and officers, almost without exception," recalled Count Benckendorff, "had their caps on, talked loudly, swearing about … The scene as was disgraceful as it could be." Upon bidding the former Tsar a final, emotional goodbye, Count Benckendorff had a foreboding: "I already feared the tragic end of this good and dear Sovereign." Benckendorff described Nicholas and Alexandra and their children as "this family of martyrs."

Among those who accompanied the family into internal exile were Pierre Gilliard, Dr. Botkin, and Alexandra's maid, Anna Demidova. When the party arrived at the train station, ready to depart, more humiliations awaited the them. The distance between the footboard of the train and the ground was great and the frail ex-Tsarina was denied a footstool to help her to board. When she did make on board at last, Alexandra, "exhausted by the effort, fell with all her weight on the floor of the compartment…"

The family journeyed grimly by train for three days in locked, dark compartments. The train lumbered eastwards toward the Ural Mountains, over thirteen hundred miles from Petrograd. When the captives arrived at Tyumen, Alexei fell, hurting his leg. He was carried onto a steamer which took the captives to Tobolsk. But before arriving there, they passed Rasputin's village and from the deck the family gathered and looked out to where Rasputin had his home. After two days on the steamer the family reached Tobolsk, a backwater town of twenty thousand inhabitants. The family were sent to live in the modest Governor's House, their latest prison.

The people of Tobolsk were sympathetic to the plight of this simple family whose head had once been the Tsar of Russia. Money problems encountered by the family prompted some of the town's merchants to smuggle provisions into the house; and peasants brought butter and eggs. When the family was allowed to attend Divine Liturgy at the Church of the Annunciation, a crowd gathered behind the soldiers. "When the family passed – the tsar and his children on foot, the empress pushed in her wheelchair – many in the crowd made the sign of the cross and some fell on their knees."

The soldiers, guarding the captives, on the other hand, were disgraceful, writing obscene messages for Olga, Tatiana, Marie, and Anastasia to see. And when Nicholas built a toboggan run out of ice and snow, the soldiers destroyed gleefully it.

As they had been when they were captives at Tsarskoe Selo, Nicholas and Alexandra maintained their calm composure at Tobolsk and tried to form some semblance of family life in Siberia despite their restricted existence. The family had been allowed to take with them, Ortipo, Tatiana's French bulldog; Jimmy, Anastasia's King Charles Spaniel; and Joy, Alexei's spaniel - pets which had provided the captives with some diversion. Lessons were begun again. Sydney Gibbes, the children's English tutor, instructed Alexei in geography and history while the former Tsarina, though suffering from poor health and was almost an invalid at only forty-five, chose to teach her children religion. Alexandra and her children also made humble, home-made Christmas presents to be sent to friends and former retainers. By now, the family had been isolated from their fellow Romanovs, a number of whom, including the former Tsar's two sisters, Olga and Xenia; Sandro; and the Dowager Empress, had fled to the Crimea.

In November, the Dowager Empress wrote to her imprisoned son, remembering how Nicholas and Alexei had visited her in Kiev, the year before: "A year has gone by already since you and darling Alexei came to see me at Kieff. Who could have thought then of all that was in store for us, and what we should have to go through. It is unbelievable."

The captives of Tobolsk were occasionally allowed to post letters to friends and family. In October 1917, Anna Viroubova received a letter from Alexandra in which the former Tsarina wrote: "In God's hands lie all things." In the following month Anna received a card from Alexei that said, "I remember you often and am very sad." Alexandra wrote to Viroubova again, telling her that she thought of Anna "so far away in loneliness and sorrow." Alexandra added that, "you know where to seek consolation and strength, and you know that God will never forsake you. His love is over all." Alexandra hoped that God "will save our unhappy country. Patience, faith and truth."

Meanwhile, events in faraway Petrograd turned more ominous. At the end of October, revolutionaries of the Left, led by Lenin, overthrew the Provisional Government. The radical Bolsheviks were now in power. Civil war soon broke out pitting the Red and White Armies against each other. The Red Army fought for the Bolsheviks while the White Armies, a loose confederation including monarchists, sought the defeat of the Communist Bolsheviks.

By the time Christmas arrived, the family's money had almost dried up thanks to the Bolshevik government who did not want to continue the financial remittances that had been granted Nicholas and Alexandra by the Provisional Government. Food supplies to the family were cut dramatically, and whatever rations they could get of eggs and milk went to Alexei. The family also suffered from the cold Siberian winter in Tobolsk. "We shiver in the rooms," wrote the former Tsarina in one letter, "and there is always a strong draught from the windows ... We all have chillbains on our fingers." By this time, the family's clothes had become threadbare so that Alexandra and her daughters mended and darned them. Yet throughout their ordeal, the family continued not to complain. Alexandra explained their attitude, telling Anna Viroubova in a letter that, "God is very near us, we feel His support, and are often amazed that we can endure events and separations which once might have killed us. Although we suffer horribly there is peace in our souls. I suffer most for Russia ..." Anna, who had been almost like another child to the former Tsarina, was not forgotten by other members of the family during their captivity, including Alexei. In one message, he wrote to Anna, telling her: "Every day I pray God we shall live together again. God bless you. Yours, A."

The former Tsarina found deep purpose in giving religious lessons to her children. "I am so contented with their souls," wrote Alexandra to Viroubova, adding about Alexei, "I hope God will bless my lessons with Baby."

And as for her husband, Alexandra was full of admiration for how he faced their ordeals. "He is simply marvelous," wrote Alexandra, "such meekness while all the time suffering intensely for his country. A real marvel." The proud mother had equally kind words for her fellow captives including her children: "The others are all good and brave and uncomplaining, and Alexei is an angel."

In an effort to improve everyone's spirits, Pierre Gilliard and Sydney Gibbes encouraged members of the family and their retainers to act in amateur plays. The weekly plays lasted into Lent of 1918. Despite these distractions, the captives could not help but note that their situation was descending into a fearful, uncertain future. The sympathies extended the family by the local villagers when they first arrived had almost disappeared as Tobolsk "grew more and more 'Sovietized.'" In February 1918, Alexandra was compelled to write that, "all is so dark and tears are flowing everywhere." But the former Tsarina also did not forget the tragedies of others, adding, "my God, how sorry I am for the innocent ones killed everywhere."

In March 1918, shocking news had reached Tobolsk that Russia's Bolshevik government had signed an agreement - the Treaty of Brest-Litovsk - with the Central Powers, ending Russia's participation in World War I. The treaty exacted a heavy, humiliating price: Russia lost a million square miles and over fifty million inhabitants, along with much of the country's industries. The former Tsarina was indignant that the Bolsheviks had chosen to do this, writing that, "our country is disintegrating into bits. I cannot think calmly about it. Such hideous pain in heart and soul." It had been a year since the Tsar had abdicated, "and the heart is wracked with pain – what has been done in one year!" lamented the former Tsarina. And to Pierre Gilliard, Alexandra said: "After what they have done to the Czar, I would rather die in Russia than be saved by the Germans!"

During this difficult time, Alexei had again caused his parents anxiety. The boy had developed a violent cough that sent him to bed. The strain of coughing caused an internal hemorrhage causing Alexei to suffer in great pain. Haunting images of Spala came to the fore. Alexandra admitted that, "I sit all day beside him, holding his aching legs, and I have grown almost as thin as he."

Soon, a Bolshevik, Commissar Vasily Yakovlev, arrived at Tobolsk with instructions to move the family to Moscow. With Alexei seriously ill and still recuperating from his hemophilia attack,

Yakovlev was then ordered to take only the former Tsar away from Tobolsk.

There is no doubt that Nicholas and Alexandra were deeply troubled. In her last letter to Anna Viroubova, the former Tsarina told her friend that, "though the storm is coming nearer and nearer, our souls are at peace." As for Pierre Gilliard, he, too, was consumed with anxiety, admitting that, "we are all in a state of anguish." Fear for the family's safety was uppermost in Gilliard's mind: "Is it possible that no one will raise a finger to save the Imperial family? Where are those who have remained loyal to the Czar? Why do they delay?"

Yakovlev then announced that he was taking Nicholas away. Yakovlev told Alexandra that she could accompany her husband if she wished. As wife and mother, Alexandra was tormented. She desperately wanted to join her husband, fearful that he might be executed, but at the same time, she could not tear herself away from her suffering son, Alexei.

"Oh, God, what ghastly torture!" Alexandra confided to Pierre Gilliard. "For the first time in my life I don't know what I ought to do."

Gilliard tried to reassure Alexandra about her son and so she finally decided, telling Gilliard that, "I'll go with the Czar; I shall trust Alexis to you…"

In explaining the situation, Alexandra told her ill son in a steady voice: "They want Papa somewhere else, and I must go with him. We'll soon be together again."

Gilliard, along with Olga, Tatiana, and Anastasia stayed on at Tobolsk to care for Alexei, who continued to endure great pain. It was Marie who accompanied Nicholas and Alexandra on to Ekaterinburg. When Nicholas and Alexandra left, Gilliard returned to Alexei's room and found the boy sobbing for his parents. His remaining sisters, too, cried torrents of tears.

The journey undertaken by Nicholas and Alexandra and their daughter, Marie, was torturous. The captives, exposed to the cold, traveled in primitive, uncomfortable carts with no springs. This meant that every bump, every jolt, every discomfort was felt and amplified. When the captives encountered a body of water that freezing cold and difficult to navigate through, Nicholas did not hesitate to come to the aid of his frail wife. He carried Alexandra uncomplainingly in his arms through the knee-deep, ice-cold water.

After more than a week of no news, the rest of the family in Tobolsk finally heard that Nicholas and Alexandra and Marie had arrived at Ekaterinburg. In May, the entire family was reunited in Ekaterinburg, the final stage of their Calvary.

Ekaterinburg at the time seethed with anti-Romanov sentiment. The city of 100,000 inhabitants had a "widespread reputation as one of the most independent and aggressively anti-monarchist territories of the new Bolshevik state." Nicholas knew this and told Yakovlev, "people there are bitterly hostile to me."

Upon arriving at Ekaterinburg, Pierre Gilliard watched as the ever-faithful Nagorny carried Alexei. Not long after, to his surprise, Gilliard was told that he and Gibbes, and Sophie Buxhoeveden were free to go. Dr. Botkin; Anna Demidova, the maid; Ivan Kharitonov, the cook, and Alexei Trupp, Nicholas's footman, remained with the family. At Ekaterinburg, Nicholas and Alexandra with their four retainers and children were imprisoned in the Ipatiev House, a white stone edifice whose windows were soon whitewashed. A fence was also built around the edifice to prevent the captives from escaping. The family's existence took a sinister tone at the Ipatiev House. Meals, when they did arrive, came from a common bowl with no utensils to use. The windows were shut so that the rooms became oppressively stifling. Water was scarce and had to be rationed. Even more harrowing were the barrage of insults and lewd comments thrown at the family by Bolshevik soldiers especially chosen for their spitefulness, extremism, and hostility toward the Romanovs. Olga, Tatiana, Marie, and Anastasia were especially subjected to crass humiliations by the soldiers. In the words of Colonel Kobylinsky, who had overseen the family's captivity at Tsarskoe Selo, the family at Ekaterinburg, was "constantly subjected to intense moral tortures."

At one point an altercation broke out between Nagorny and a soldier who had coveted a small gold chain hung with icons that hung over the sickbed of Alexei. When the soldier snatched the chain, an outraged Nagorny tried to stop him. For his loyalty to Alexei, Nagorny was shot dead.

Alexei's frail condition worried his family. He lay in bed with a high temperature and was continually in pain from his hemophilia attack. Alexandra's sparse, concise entries in her final diary are peppered with references to Alexei's state of health. In May her entry read: "Baby woke up every hour pain in his knee, slipped & hurt it when getting into bed. – Cannot walk yet, one carries him. Lost 14 pounds since his illness." The next day, Alexandra wrote, "Baby had bad night again." Four days later: "Baby was carried to his bed to his room again. Pains stronger."

Throughout the family's agonizing ordeal in the Ipatiev House, they remained united and strong in their faith. The family's religiosity, courage, and dignity in the face of their deprivations and insults had moved at least one guard, Anatoly Yakimov, to pity them. He later recalled how he got the impression that Nicholas was "a kind, modest, frank and talkative person." Yakimov added of the family: "After I personally saw them several times I began to feel entirely different towards them: I began to pity them. I pitied them as human beings. I had the idea in my head to let them escape, or to do something to allow them to escape." Escape, however, was denied them.

In mid-July, the family seemed almost to have a premonition that something terrible was about to happen. Two priests who said Divine Liturgy at the Ipatiev House could sense this. One of them, Father Storozhev, noted that Alexei looked pale as he sat in his wheelchair. When the priests began to chant: "Who Resteth with the Saints," a prayer meant for dead souls, the family fell on their knees, "as though it were a requiem," so overcome were they with emotion. After the service, Father Storozhev spoke with his colleague who had assisted. "Do you know, Father Archpresbyter," said the assistant priest, "something has happened to them there."

By July, Russia was gripped in civil war, pitting the Bolshevik Red Army against the monarchist White Armies. The Whites threatened Ekaterinburg. This, in turn, tightened the Boshevik vise on the former imperial family, for the question of what to do with the former Tsar and his family had taken on great significance. Already in June, the former Tsar's brother, Michael, had been shot to death in Perm. Lenin, in Moscow, harbored a hatred of the Romanovs. He gave the final order that sealed the family's fate: execution, with no one spared.

In the early hours of July 16, 1918, the family was awakened and sent into the basement of the Ipatiev House. Accompanying the family were their loyal retainers: Dr. Botkin, Anna Demidova, Alexei Trupp, and Ivan Kharitonov. Nicholas carried Alexei in his arms then put his son on one chair while Alexandra sat on another. Yakov Yurovsky, a loyal Bolshevik, led his squad of executioners into the basement of the Ipatiev House.

"Nicholas Alexandrovitch, your relatives are trying to save you, therefore we are compelled to shoot you," declared Yurovsky.

Nicholas tried to protect his wife and son but was shot by Yurovsky. Alexandra crossed herself. Several of the women cried. For several minutes a savage scene unfolded as the executioners fired, some of the bullets ricocheting through the basement. When the shooting finally stopped, Alexei was still alive, his father's dead body having shielded him from the barrage of bullets. The poor boy struggled across the floor, covered in blood. Yurovsky shot him dead. Three of his sisters had survived, but then were shot at again and stabbed with bayonets. The brutal massacre took twenty minutes.

The savage end of Nicholas and Alexandra and their children is all the more tragic in view of the close, loving relationship they felt for each other. Pierre Gilliard wrote of the family's "nobility of mind and the wonderful moral grandeur they displayed through all their suffering." In his deposition, Colonel Kobylinsky, who had overseen the imperial family's captivity at Tsarskoe Selo, admitted that he had been moved by what he saw of the family during their captivity. "They all loved each other" concluded Kobylinsky, and that, "never before in my life have I seen, and probably never again shall see, such a good, friendly and agreeable family." And as for Alexei, the child of his parents' many prayers, Kobylinsky noted that, "the czarevitch was the idol of the whole family."

The fact that Alexei was Nicholas and Alexandra's only son and heir marked the Tsarevich as special from the moment of his birth. But his hemophilia, which he endured with great patience, and the ensuing tragedies attached to it and to his family, turned Alexei Nikolaevich Romanov into "one of the most tragic figures in history," as Anna Viroubova rightly described him. Others, who were equally close to the imperial family as Viroubova had been, made similar observations of the young boy whose life had been cut short in a hail of bullets. Of Alexei, Sydney Gibbes declared that, "he suffered much in his childhood," but "had a kind heart … was a clever boy … [whose] mother loved him passionately." Pierre Gilliard wrote that, "the illness of the Czarevitch cast its shadow over the whole of the concluding period of the Czar Nicholas II's reign … it was one of the main causes of his fall, for it made possible the phenomenon of Rasputin and resulted in the fatal isolation of the sovereigns who lived in a world apart, wholly absorbed in a tragic anxiety which had to be concealed from all eyes." It was Sophie Buxhoeveden, however, who best summed up in poignant words the life of the Tsarevich Alexei: "All he suffered in the course of his short life can scarcely be believed. It did not embitter him. It only seemed to give him a pity, unusual in a child, for the suffering of other people."

The historian Robert K. Massie, in his classic account of the last years of imperial Russia, *Nicholas and Alexandra*, eloquently wrote of the impact the Tsarevich Alexei's hemophilia had upon his family, upon Russia, and beyond:

> *It is one of the supreme ironies of history that the blessed birth of an only son should have proved the mortal blow. Even as the saluting cannons boomed and the flags waved, Fate had prepared a terrible story. Along with the lost battles and sunken ships, the bombs, the revolutionaries and their plots, the strikes and revolts, Imperial Russia was toppled by a tiny defect in the body of a little boy. Hidden from public view, veiled in rumor, working from within, this unseen tragedy would change the history of Russia and the world.*

EPILOGUE

Since the fall of the Soviet Union in 1991, Tsar Nicholas II, Tsarina Alexandra, their children, and the Romanov dynasty as a whole have undergone renewed popularity in Russia. Statues and plaques in honor of the family and other Romanovs have been erected, exhibitions on them have been mounted and well-attended.

The Ipatiev House was razed in 1977 and in its place, the Church on the Blood was erected. Beneath the altar of the church is the site of the execution of Nicholas, Alexandra, their five children, and retainers. Several miles from Ekaterinburg, at Ganina Yama, seven chapels have been erected on the site representing each of the Romanovs killed. This place, now known as the Monastery of the Holy Imperial Passion Bearers is where the bodies of the victims of the Ipatiev House massacre were first buried.

Tsar's Days are held in Ekaterinburg in July each year in commemoration of the imperial family.

Participation has grown with each passing year. In July 2018, on the 100th anniversary of the execution of the imperial family, 200,000 people participated in Tsar's Days. The three-day commemoration involves prayers, veneration, and processions. A long vigil is held at the Church on the Blood on the night of July 16th. This is followed by a four-hour procession to Ganina Yama. Many of the pilgrims carry banners and icons of the imperial family during the procession.

In 2000, the Moscow Patriarchate canonized Tsar Nicholas II, Tsarina Alexandra, and their children as passion bearers and as such, the last imperial family of tsarist Russia is viewed by the faithful as martyrs and thus worthy of veneration

.

Did you enjoy this book?

I hope you enjoyed reading this book. If you did, I would be most grateful if you could please post a brief review on Amazon.

Please see my other books on the Royal Cavalcade series as well. I hope you will find another book or several books from the series which you may come to enjoy. I welcome hearing from my readers. You may reach me via my website at: www.juliapgelardi.com.

ENDNOTES

Chapter 1:

"I am extremely .... belonged to Russia.": *Munsey's Magazine*, vol. XXIII, no. 3, June 1905, p. 352.

"My God, it is .... the nation say?": Marfa Mouchanow, *My Empress* (New York: John Lane Company, 1918), p. 91.

"What good does .... heir to Russia!": *Ibid.*, p. 90.

"You will someday .... you of God.": Robert K. Massie, *Nicholas and Alexandra* (New York: Atheneum, 1967), p. 198.

"I congratulate Your Majesty .... of a Czarevitsch.": Mouchanow, *My Empress*, p. 155.

"Oh, it cannot .... really a boy?": *Ibid.*

"A great and ..... grace of God": Diary entry of Tsar Nicholas II, 30 July 1904 in Andrei Maylunas and Sergei Mironenko, eds., *A Lifelong Passion: Nicholas and Alexandra, Their Own Story* (London: Weidenfeld & Nicolson, 1996), p. 243.

"There are no words .... of sore trials!": *Ibid.*

"it absorbed for …. the Far East." Mouchanow, *My Empress*, p. 155.

"wildest rejoicings …. over the Empire.": Anna Viroubova, *Memories of the Russian Court* (London: Macmillan and Co., Ltd., 1923), p. 10.

"how happy the …. news was announced.": Memoirs of Grand Duchess Olga Alexandrovna in Maylunas and Mironenko, *A Lifelong Passion*, p. 241.

"God has sent …. it has happened.": Diary entry of Grand Duke Konstantin Konstantinovich, 11 August 1904 in *Ibid.*, p. 245.

"the little sisters …. critical remarks about him.": M. Eagar, *Six Years at the Russian Court* (London: Hurst and Blackett, Ltd., 1906), pp. 281-2.

"In the middle …. years to come." *Ibid.*, pp. 282-3.

"a real Sunbeam …. can help you…": Tsarina Alexandra to Tsar Nicholas II, 15 August 1904 in Maylunas and Mironenko, *A Lifelong Passion*, p. 245.

"Oh God is indeed …. is a big." Tsarina Alexandra to Tsar Nicholas II, undated in *Ibid.*, p. 246.

"chubby, rosy – a wonderful boy!": A. A. Mossolov, *At the Court of the Last Tsar: Being the Memoirs of A.A. Mossolov, Head of the Court Chancellery, 1900-1916*. Edited by A.A. Pilenco. Translated by E.W. Dickes (London: Methuen & Co., Ltd., 1935), p. 29.

"he's an amazingly .... a warrior knight.": Diary entry of Grand Duchess Xenia, 16 August 1904 in Maylunas and Mironenko, *A Lifelong Passion*, p. 245.

"he is a very beautiful boy.": Eagar, *Six Years*, p. 282.

Chapter 2:

"Alix and I were very worried...": Diary entry of Tsar Nicholas II, 8 September 1904 in Maylunas and Mironenko, *A Lifelong Passion*, p. 247.

"with the calmest .... haemophilia." Helen Rappaport, *The Romanov Sisters: The Lost Lives of the Daughters of Nicholas and Alexandra* (New York: St. Martin's Press, 2014), pp. 79-80.

"from that moment .... as moral altered.": Grand Duchess Marie, *Education of a Princess: A Memoir* (New York: Blue Ribbon Books, Inc., 1933), p. 61.

"He could not …. of an invalid.": Grand Duke Alexander, *Once a Grand Duke* (New York: Cosmopolitan Book Corporation, 1932). p. 183.

"has always been a remarkably healthy child.": *The Sphere*, Vol. XX, No. 265, February 18, 1905.

"the Czar is immensely proud….": *Ibid.*

"Don't you think …. He's well nourished!": Mossolov. *Court of the Last Tsar*, p. 30.

"he can walk quite well…": Tsar Nicholas II to the Dowager Empress Marie Feodorovna, 1st December 1905 in Edward J. Bing, ed., *The Secret Letters of the Last Tsar: Being the Confidential Correspondence Between Nicholas II and His Mother, Dowager Empress Maria Feodorovona* (New York: Longmans, Green, and Co., 1938), p. 195.

"the Empress's favourite …. was her boy.": Baroness Sophie Buxhoeveden, *The Life & Tragedy of Alexandra Feodorovna* (London: Longmans, Green and Co., 1929), p. 150.

"quiet home life …. peace and happiness" *Munsey's Magazine*, vol. XXIII, no. 3, June 1905, p. 352.

"Nicholas II, failing to …. Grand Duke Sergei Alexandrovich.": John Curtis Perry and

Constantine Pleshakov, *Flight of the Romanovs: A Family Saga* (New York: Basic Books, 1999), p. 92.

"These terrible events .... to unknown fortunes.": Harrison E. Salibury, *Black Night, White Snow: Russia's Revolutions 1905*-1917, London: Cassell, 1977), p. 136.

"a powerful icon ..... the Black Sea fleet.": Perry and Pleshakov, *Flight of the Romanovs*, p. 94.

"It makes me .... riots, disorders, mutinies.": Tsar Nicholas II to Dowager Empress Marie Feodorovna, 19th October 1905 in Bing, *Secret Letters of the Last Tsar*, p. 183.

"few countries have .... The Middle Ages.": Salibury, *Black Night, White Snow*, p. 155.

"a feeling of .... at the court.": Abraham Yarmolinsky, ed. and transl., *The Memoirs of Count Witte* (Garden City, NY: Doubleday, Page & Company, 1921), p. 312.

"crush the rebellion .... be a constitution.": Tsar Nicholas II to Dowager Empress Marie Feodorovna, 19th October 1905 in Bing, *Secret Letters of the Tsar*, p. 184.

"many Russians (also) …. only with reluctance.": Perry and Pleshakov, *Flight of the Romanovs*, p. 96.

"would be a great hindrance": Yarmolinsky, *Memoirs of Count Witte*, p. 313.

Chapter 3:

"the dynasty enjoyed …. throne of bayonets.": Perry and Pleshakov, *Flight of the Romanovs*, p. 96.

"high spirited …. full of fun": Mouchanow, *My Empress*, p. 159.

"How do you …. talk with you.": Gleb Botkin, *The Real Romanovs: As Revealed by the Late Czar's Physician and His Son* (New York: Fleming H. Revell Company, 1931), p. 32.

"his illness was …. to be falling.: Buxhoeveden, *Life & Tragedy*, p. 151.

"the birth of …. their heaviest cross…": Ian Vorres, *The Last Grand Duchess: Her Imperial Highness Grand Duchess Olga Alexandrovna* (New York: Charles Scriber's Sons, 1964), p. 119.

"most painful to …. state of health.": Mouchanow, *My Empress*, p. 158.

"I could see …. struck at once.": Pierre Gilliard, *Thirteen Years at the Russian Court* (New York: George H. Doran & Co., 1921), p. 26.

"in such pain …. leg terribly swollen." Vorres, *Last Grand Duchess*, p. 139.

"Poor boy it …. suffered from it.": Dowager Empress Marie Feodorovna to Tsar Nicholas II, 7th March 1908 in Bing, *Secret Letters of the Last Tsar*, p. 231.

"The combination of …. on any child.": Robert K. Massie, *Nicholas and Alexandra* (New York: Atheneum, 1967), p. 138.

"warm my hands …. pain-racked limbs.": Viroubova, *Memories of the Russian Court*, p. 81.

"Can't I have …. and I nothing?": *Ibid.*, pp. 81-2.

"to the Empress …. end of time." Lili Dehn, *The Real Tsaritsa* (Boston: Little, Brown, and Company, 1922), p. 82.

"gift of noise …. impertinence of Anastasia.": Botkin, *Real Romanovs*, p. 28.

"to whom the …. very heart's blood": Viroubova, *Memories of the Russian Court*, p. 83.

"Everybody in the …. and pitied him.": Botkin, *Real Romanovs*, p. 28.

"enormous difficulties. Scarcely .... diligence and concentration.": Mossolov, *Court of the Last Tsar*, p. 54.

"a good memory .... lost time.": Buxhoeveden, *Life & Tragedy*, p. 151.

"child of many prayers" .... "adored him.": Dehn, *Real Tsaritsa*, p. 81.

"because of the frequent .... Suffering excruciating pains.": Botkin, *Real Romanovs*, p. 28.

Chapter 4:

"the Empress saw .... hour of need.": Buxhoeveden, *Life & Tragedy*, p. 138.

"determined to wrest .... which science denied.": Massie, *Nicholas and Alexandra*, p. 154.

"A few days ago .... more than an hour.": Tsar Nicholas II to Peter Stolypin, 16 October 1906 in Maylunas and Mironenko, *A Lifelong Passion*, p. 296.

"spent the whole .... us about Grigory.": Diary entry of Nicholas II, 19 December 1906 in *Ibid.*, p. 297.

"The little boy .... on his leg.": Vorres, *Last Grand Duchess*, p. 139.

"Rasputin had incontestable .... he managed it.": Mossolov, *Court of the Last Tsar*, p. 148.

"sincerely thought that .... and ignorant people..'": Mouchanow, *My Empress*, p. 186.

"the Imperial Family .... Or any other's.": Viroubova, *Memories of the Russian Court*, p. 82.

"there are people .... incurable by the doctors.": N.P. Sabline memoirs in Maylunas and Mironenko, *A Lifelong Passion*, pp. 314-15.

"instantly struck by .... one's inmost thoughts.": Dehn, *Real Tsaritsa*, p. 101.

"possessed hypnotic and .... others do so.": *Ibid.*, p. 126.

"seemed to be constantly .... being looked at.": Prince Felix Youssoupoff, *Lost Splendor* (New York: G.P. Putnam's Sons), pp. 140-1.

"was just beginning .... in my power." *Ibid.*, pp. 201-2.

"Believe in the .... son will live!": Gilliard, *Thirteen Years*, p. 52.

"Rasputin had realised .... advantage from it": *Ibid.*, p. 53.

"felt that gentleness .... to like him.": Vorres, *Last Grand Duchess*, p. 134.

"would never have .... was always respectful.":
Ibid., p. 136.

"Rasputin's influence over .... was purely mystical.": Dehn, *Real Tsaritsa*, p. 103.

"there may have .... at Tsarskoe Selo.": *Ibid.*, p. 107.

"because of his ... a fatal mistake.": Botkin, *Real Romanovs*, p. 60.

"I believe in Rasputin.": Dehn, *Real Tsaritsa*, p. 105.

"the nursery was .... all Russia's troubles.": Bernard Pares, *The Fall of the Russian Monarchy: A Study of the Evidence* (London: Jonathan Cape, 1939), p. 16.

"I was absolutely .... is terrible, terrible.": Mikhail Rodzianko, *The Reign of Rasputin: An Empire's Collapse* (London: A.M. Philpot Ltd., 1927), p. 37.

Chapter 5:
"a long, finely-chiselled .... happy, romping boy.": Gilliard, *Thirteen Years*, p. 40.

"was making a .... caused serious accidents.": *Ibid.*, p. 85.

"Alexei got hold …. our great surprise.": Tsar Nicholas II to Dowager Empress Marie, 10th September, 1912 in Bing, *Secret Letters of the Tsar*, p. 274.

"the next weeks …. about our duties.": Viroubova, *Memories of the Russian Court*, p. 92.

"growing thinner and …. wan, drawn face.": Buxhoeveden, *Life & Tragedy*, p. 131.

"was absolutely bloodless …. in the wood.": Viroubova, *Memories of the Russian Court*, p. 93.

"The poor darling …. mercy upon me.'": Tsar Nicholas II to Dowager Empress Marie, 10th September, 1912 in Bing, *Secret Letters of the Tsar*, p. 276.

"The anxiety of …. was beyond description.": Mossolov, *Court of the Last Tsar*, p. 150.

"they could do nothing more.": Buxhoeveden, *Life & Tragedy*, p. 133.

"There was a …. God protect him!'": Diary entry of Grand Duke Konstantin Konstantinovich, 9 October 1912 in Maylunas and Mironenko, *A Lifelong Passion*, p. 357.

"The little one will not die.": Viroubova, *Memories of the Russian Court*, p. 94.

"allowed to be .... haemorrhage has stopped.": Mossolov, *Court of the Last Tsar* p. 151.

"an abdominal hemorrhage .... on the nerve.": Royal Paediatrician Rakhfus, Royal Surgeon Fedorov, His Majesty's Royal Physician Ev. Botkin, Honourable Royal Physicain S. Ostrogorsky, "Announcement by the Minister of the Imperial Court," 21 October 1912 in Maylunas and Mironenko, *A Lifelong Passion*, pp. 359-360.

"my heart [is] filled .... dear Alexey's recovery.": Tsar Nicholas II to Dowager Empress Marie Feodorovna, 20th October 1912, Bing, *Secret Letters of the Last Tsar*, p. 275.

"After 1912, when .... to his sanctity.": Buxhoeveden, *Life & Tragedy*, p. 142.

"the Tsar of .... Russia of 1913." R.H. Bruce Lockhart in Bing, *Secret Letters of the Last Tsar*, p. 10.

"intended to be a national rejoicing," Rodzianko, *Reign of Rasputin*, p. 75.

"I felt myself .... placed than you": *Ibid.*, pp. 76-7.

"thin crowds and .... young grand duchesses.": Greg King, *The Last Empress: The Life & Ties of*

Alexandra Feodorovna, Tsarina of Russia (New York: Birch Lane Press, 1994), p. 202.

"But for all …. little real loyalty.": Viroubova, *Memories of the Russian Court*, p. 99.

"I was so …. am a wreck.": *Ibid.*, p. 100.

Chapter 6:

"they should realise …. all this beauty." Buxhoeveden, *Life & Tragedy*, p. 180.

"he had grown …. in high spirits.": Gilliard, *Thirteen Years*, p. 91.

"I prefer to …. endure perpetual scenes.": Catherine Radziwill, *Nicholas II: The Last of the Tsars* (London: Cassell and Company Ltd., 1931), p. 194.

"I would gladly … kill that scoundrel!": Youssoupoff, *Lost Splendor*, p. 203.

"If you forsake …. within six months." Gilliard, *Thirteen Years*, p. 204.

"very handsome but …. perfect good grace": Marie, Queen of Roumania, *The Story of My Life* (New York: Charles Scribner's Sons, 1934), p. 582.

"making brave efforts …. was very flushed." *Ibid.*, p. 581.

"The great wave …. a visitation by God…": Perry and Pleshakov, *Flight of the Romanovs*, pp. 109-110.

"weeping in disappointment …. lead us to victory!": Massie, *Nicholas and Alexandra*, p. 277.

"in despair …. to pursue him." Gilliard, *Thirteen Years*, p. 113.

"The Heir! …. touched the Heir!" *Ibid.*, p. 115.

"It will be …. through ghastly sufferings.": Buxhoeveden, *Life & Tragedy*, p. 189.

"a menacing cloud …. end the grief.": Massie, *Nicholas and Alexandra*, p. 282.

"Do come! I will hang you!": Sir George Buchanan, *My Mission to Russia and Other Diplomatic Memories, Volume I* (London: Cassell and Company, 1923), p. 239.

"Toward this step …. of overweening ambitions.": Grand Duchess Marie, *Education of a Princess*, p. 222.

"the appearance of …. would further bolster": Massie, *Nicholas and Alexandra*, p. 298.

"Dear Papa …. Your loving Alexei": Tsarevich Alexei to Tsar Nicholas II, 24 November 1914 in Maylunas and Mironenko, *A Lifelong Passion*, p. 410.

"Dear Mama I .... Your Alexei.": Tsarevich Alexei to Tsarina Alexandra, 18 May 1916 in *Ibid.*, p. 467.

"Dearest darling Mama ..... son and brother.": Tsarevich Alexei to Tsarina Alexandra, 15 October 1916 in *Ibid.*, p. 476.

"The Little One's presence .... about near-by.": Radziwill, *Nicholas II*, p. 251.

"the Heir-Apparent .... a happy reign.": Count Paul Benckendorff, *Last Days at Tsarskoe Selo: Being the Personal Notes and Memories of Count Paul Benckendorff, Telling of the Last Sojourn of the Emperor & Empress of Russia at Tsarskoe Selo from March 1 to August 1, 1917*. Translated by Maurice Baring (London: William Heinemann Limited, 1927), pp. 115-116.

"Baby played the .... at the nose.": Radziwill, *Nicholas II*, p. 252.

"was particularly harrowing .... end had come.": Gilliard, *Thirteen Years*, p. 156.

"never forget the .... Nothing will happen.": Viroubova, *Memories of the Russian Court*, p. 169.

"Alexei is recovering .... going without him.": Tsar Nicholas II to Dowager Empress Marie

Feodorovna, 12th December 1915, Bing, *Secret Letters of the Tsar*, p. 297.

"harken unto our …. advice – is great.": Tsarina Alexandra to Tsar Nicholas II, 10 June 1915 in Maylunas and Mironenko, *A Lifelong Passion*, p. 426.

"The illness of the Czarevitch …. from all eyes.": Gilliard, *Thirteen Years*, p. viii.

"he spoke so …. three hundred years!": Radziwill, *Nicholas II*, p. 193.

"I am but … ones on earth…": Salisbury, *Black Night, White Snow*, p. 283.

"broken all the …. her with Germany." Buchanan, *My Mission to Russia, Vol. I*, p. 245.

"I knew her …. fervent Russian patriotism.": Grand Duke Alexander, *Once a Grand Duke*, pp. 270-1.

"shake Nicky by …. but my wife,": *Ibid.*, p. 275.

"intrigues of every …. like poisonous fungi.": Mossolov, *Court of the Last Tsar*, p. 161.

"the conduct of …. Emperor and Empress.": Buchanan, *My Mission to Russia, Vol. I*, p. 245.

"the Empress devoted …. desiring a separate peace.": Grand Duchess Marie, *Education of a Princess*, p. 219.

"Remember the fate .... and Marie Antoinette.":
Salisbury, *Black Night, White Snow*, p. 291.

"This is not .... is all her.": *Ibid.*, p. 285.

"simply despised him.": Grand Duchess Marie,
Education of a Princess, p. 241.

"she was driving .... must be annihilated.":
Rodzianko, *Reign of Rasputin*, pp. 246-7.

"The Press began .... of the Empress.":
Mossolov, *Court of the Last Tsar*, p. 176.

"almost a saint ... warnings given her." Meriel
Buchanan, *Recollections of Imperial Russia*
(London: Hutchinson & Co., 1923), p. 256.

"it was about .... baffling, almost incredible.":
Grand Duchess Marie, *Education of a Princess*, pp.
248-9.

"the war had .... were growing apace.": Pares,
Fall of the Russian Monarchy, p. 301.

"incorruptible man of the people.": Richard
Pipes, *The Russian Revolution* (New York: Vintage
Books, 1991), p. 262.

"He [Rasputin] entreats you .... up all again.":
Tsarina Alexandra to Tsar Nicholas II, 13
December 1916 in Maylunas and Mironenko, *A
Lifelong Passion*, p. 490.

"the Tsarevitch, with .... get him away...": Princess Paley, *Memories of Russia 1916-1919* (London: Herbert Jenkins Ltd., 1924), pp. 21-2.

"Remove Rasputin.": Salisbury, *Black Night, White Snow*, p. 295.

"I don't care .... only harming themselves.": Youssoupoff, *Lost Splendor*, p. 215.

"I felt as .... administered to me.": *Ibid.*, p. 218.

"Now, see, you're .... and terrible struggle.": *Ibid.*, p. 237.

"our hearts were .... ruin and dishonor.": *Ibid.*, p. 241.

"Felix, Felix. .... to the Czarina.": Salisbury, *Black Night, White Snow*, p. 305.

"I cannot & *won't* believe it.": Pipes, *Russian Revolution*, p. 265.

"the Empress is .... her at once.": Maurice Paléologue, *An Ambassador's Memoirs, Volume III*. Translated by F.A. Holt (New York: George H. Doran Company, 1923), p. 132.

"I did not .... sense of relief.": Pipes, *Russian Revolution*, p. 266.

"my heart perceived her torture.": Grand Duchess Marie, *Education of a Princess*, p. 271.

"misguided patriots .... grand duke or peasant?":
Grand Duke Alexander, *Once a Grand Duke*, p.
279.

"the Tsar saw .... and his wife.": Mossolov,
Court of the Last Tsar, p. 98.

"Forgetting himself, he .... to realize that?":
Grand Duchess Marie, *Education of a Princess*, p,
p. 271.

"I do not permit .... clean conscience either.":
Tsar Nicholas II, in Bing, *Secret Letters of the Last
Tsar*, p. 301.

"Nobody has a right of assassination!":
Mossolov, *Court of the Last Tsar*, p. 98.

"she felt sad .... felt were numbered."."":
Buxhoeveden, *Life & Tragedy*, p. 244.

"If I die .... within six months.": Diary entry of
February 11, 1917 in Paléologue, *An Ambassador's
Memoirs, Vol. III*, p. 191.

Chapter 7:

"their explanation of .... before the Tsar.": Diary
entry of February 11, 1917 in Paléologue, *An
Ambassador's Memoirs, Vol. III*, p. 191.

"we were toasted .... uttered dire threats.":
Youssoupoff, *Lost Splendor*, p. 261.

"one of them …. the bitter end.": Gilliard, *Thirteen Years*, p. 189.

"toward the end …. struggle against destiny.": Youssoupoff, *Lost Splendor*, p. 260.

"I fear that …. its last safeguard.": Diary entry of January 10, 1917 in Paléologue, *An Ambassador's Memoirs, Vol. III*, p. 159.

"understood nothing, knew …. Death of a Nation.": Grand Duke Alexander, *Once a Grand Duke*, p. 280.

"The Empress is …. make her respected!": January 25, 1917 in Paléologue, *An Ambassador's Memoirs, Vol. III*, p. 172.

"I can only …. our dear Russia.": Dowager Empress Marie Feodorovna to Tsar Nicholas II, 17th February 1917 in Bing, undated, *Secret Letters of the Last Tsar*, p. 302.

"Is it possible …. all a mistake?": Pipes, *Russian Revolution*, p. 269.

"many gifts that …. came near him.": Buchanan, *My Mission to Russia, Vol. II*, p. 77.

"He was very …. he entirely lacked.": Benckendorff, *Last Days at Tsarskoe*, pp. 113-14.

"was certain that …. would be his.": Gilliard, *Thirteen Years*, p. 193.

"grew daily more depressing.": Youssoupoff, *Lost Splendor*, p. 272.

"breach in the stronghold of Czarism.": Salisbury, *Black Night, White Snow*, p. 350.

"It's a revolting .... of bad news!": Diary entry of Tsar Nicholas II, 27 February 1917 in Maylunas and Mironenko, *A Lifelong Passion*, p. 540.

"the revolution, which .... in the town.": Benckendorff, *Last Days at Tsarskoe Selo*, p. 1.

"dying of hunger .... few more hours.": *Ibid.*, p. 4.

"I don't want .... truth from them...": Dehn, *Real Tsaritsa*, p. 152.

"lying desperately ill .... spectre of Revolution!": *Ibid.*, p. 155.

"This sounds a .... verge of fainting.": *Ibid.*, p. 160.

"could scarcely master her anxiety.": Buxhoeveden, *Life & Tragedy*, p. 252.

"They intended to .... Staff at Petrograd.": *Ibid.*, p. 254.

"how well she .... was unforgettable.": *Ibid.*, pp. 254-5.

"the vast dark .... the empty rooms.": *Ibid.*, p. 256.

"My sailors .... can't believe it.": Dehn, *Real Tsaritsa*, p. 162.

"Otherwise anarchy would .... in the extreme.": Radziwill, *Nicholas II*, p. 297.

"I must on my .... heritage to him.": Perry and Pleshakov, *Flight of the Romanovs*, p. 152.

"too late.": Sir George Buchanan, *My Mission to Russia and Other Diplomatic Memoirs, Volume II* (London: Cassell and Company, Ltd., 1923), p. 68.

"does not enjoy .... valley of Josaphat.": Diary entry of January 31, 1917 in Paléologue, *An Ambassador's Memoirs*, *Vol. III*, p. 181.

"Tell me frankly .... keep him ourselves." Gilliard, *Thirteen Years*, pp. 195-6.

"shall I be .... such a thing.": Radziwill, *Nicholas II*, pp. 300-1.

"I hope you .... the monarchist state.": Rosemary and Donald Crawford, *Michael and Natasha: The Life and Love of the Last Tsar of Russia* (Vancouver: Douglas & McIntyre, 1997), pp. 286-7.

"was master of .... willing accepter of defeat.": Pares, *Fall of the Russian Monarchy*, p. 467.

"The destiny of .... God help Russia!": *Ibid.*, pp. 467-8.

"the immediate accession .... make him abdicate.": Diary entry of March 18, 1917 in Paléologue, *An Ambassador's Memoirs, Vol. III*, p. 251.

"an event of gigantic significance.": Massie, *Nicholas and Alexandra*, p. 418.

"noticed how those .... cowardice and deceit.": Pares, *Fall of the Russian Monarchy*, p. 469.

"had so quickly .... us like treason.": Benckendorff, *Last Days at Tsarskoe Selo*, p. 44.

"the decision of .... take that step.": Grand Duchess Marie, *Education of a Princess*, p. 289.

"aroused the fury .... 'No more Romanovs!'": Diary entry of March 16, 1917 in Paléologue, *An Ambassador's Memoirs, Vol. III*, p. 238.

"very dismal .... events are taking.": Diary entry of March 17, 1917 in *Ibid.*, p. 239.

"her calm and the serenity of her gaze.": Princess Paley, *Memories of Russia*, p. 61.

"signed his abdication .... and my hospital.": *Ibid.*

"Her face was .... *Abdiqué!*": Dehn, *Real Tsaritsa*, p. 165.

"Now *he'll* be .... away her son!": *Ibid.*, p. 167.

"You know your …. as the Heir.": Gilliard, *Thirteen Years*, p. 215.

"Shall I never …. to us now.": Dehn, *Real Tsaritsa*, p. 183.

Chapter 8:

"wept bitterly …. she had shared.": Dehn, *Real Tsaritsa*, p. 191.

"except when he …. light-hearted child.": *Ibid.*, p. 205.

"you are the noblest of men!": Diary entry of March 17, 1917 in Paléologue, *An Ambassador's Memoirs, Vol. III*, p. 241.

"the prisoners had …. day that passed.": Radziwill, *Nicholas II*, p. 304.

"from this time …. to the end.": Pares, *Fall of the Russian Monarchy*, p. 412.

"she lost none …. the Imperial Family.": Viroubova, *Memories of the Russian Court*, p. 206.

"Enemies of the Revolution …. Ah, never, never…": Grand Duke Alexander, *Once a Grand Duke*, p. 296.

"Where is the …. us the Heir?": Vladimir A. Kozlov and Vladimir M. Khrustalëv, eds., *The Last*

Diary of Tsaritsa Alexandra (New Haven, CT: Yale University Press), p. xx.

"the soldiers – with …. speak to them.": Benckendorff, *Last Days at Tsarskoe Selo*, p. 84.

"Well, well, Nicolouchka …. resignation so great": Princess Paley, *Memories of Russia*, p. 87.

"the most united …. of her words.": Benckendorff, *Last Days at Tsarskoe Selo*, pp. 75-6.

"your wife does not lie.": Buxhoeveden, *Life & Tragedy*, p. 282.

"learned that they …. compelled to admire.": E.M. Almedingen, *The Empress Alexandra 1872-1918: A Study* (London: Hutchinson, 1961), p. 211.

"One can find …. love Him undescribable joy.": Dehn, *Real Tsaritsa*, p. 239.

"at this day dear to me.": *Ibid.*, p. 240.

"the ceremony was …. to come back.": Benckendorff, *Last Days at Tsarskoe Selo*, pp. 103-4.

"enjoyed acting as …. are at present!": *Ibid.*, p. 96.

"smells of blood …. one word – revolution.": Perry and Pleshakov, *Flight of the Romanovs*, p. 185.

"Time had been …. a Siberian exile.": Grand Duke Alexander, *Once a Grand Duke*, p. 297.

"The soldiers and …. it could be.": Benckendorff, *Last Days at Tsarskoe Selo*, p. 108.

"I already feared …. and dear Sovereign.": *Ibid.*, p. 110.

"this family of martyrs.": *Ibid.*, p. 112.

"exhausted by the …. of the compartment…": Paley, *Memories of Russia*, p. 108.

"When the family …. on their knees." Robert K. Massie introduction in Kozlov and Khrustalëv, *Last Diary*, p. xxv.

"A year has …. It is unbelievable.": Dowager Empress Marie Feodorovna to Nicholas, Aitodor, 21st November 1917 in Bing, *Secret Letters of the Tsar*, pp. 303-4.

"In God's hands lie all things.": Viroubova, *Memories of the Russian Court*, p. 298.

"I remember you …. am very sad.": *Ibid.*, p. 300.

"so far away …. faith and truth.": *Ibid.*

"We shiver in …. on our fingers.": *Ibid.*, p. 302.

"God is very …. most for Russia …": *Ibid.*, p. 305.

"Every day I …. Yours, A.": *Ibid.*, p. 308.

"I am so .... is an angel.": *Ibid.*, pp. 311-12.

"grew more and more 'Sovietized.'": Almedingen, *Empress Alexandra*, p. 220.

"all is so dark .... ones killed everywhere.": Viroubova, *Memories of the Russian Court*, p. 332.

"our country is .... heart and soul.": *Ibid.*, p. 335.

"and the heart .... in one year!": Dehn, *Real Tsaritsa*, p. 245.

"After what they ... by the Germans!": Gilliard, *Thirteen Years*, p. 257.

"I sit all .... thin as he.": Viroubova, *Memories of the Russian Court*, p. 338.

"though the storm .... are at peace.": *Ibid.*, p. 342.

"we are all .... do they delay?": Gilliard, *Thirteen Years*, p. 260.

"Oh, God, what .... Alexis to you...": *Ibid.*, p. 261.

"They want Papa .... be together again.": Almedingen, *Empress Alexandra*, p. 224.

"widespread reputation as .... hostile to me.": Massie introduction in Kozlov and Khrustalëv, *Last Diary*, p. xxxvi.

"constantly subjected to intense moral tortures.":
Deposition of Colonel Kobylinsky in George
Gustav Telberg and Robert Wilton, *The Last Days
of the Romanovs* (New York: George H. Doran
Company, 1920), p. 129.

"Baby woke up …. since his illness.": Diary
entry of Alexandra Feodorovna,10/23 May 1918 in
Kozlov and Khrustalёv, *Last Diary*, p. 144.

"Baby had bad night again.": Diary entry of
Alexandra Feodorovna, 11/24 May 1918 in *Ibid.*, p.
145.

"Baby was carried …. Pains stronger.": Diary
entry of Alexandra Feodorovna, 15/28 May 1918 in
Ibid., p. 149.

"a kind, modest, frank and talkative person.":
Deposition of Anatolie Iakimoff in Telberg and
Wilton, *Last Days*, p. 181.

"After I personally …. them to escape.": *Ibid.*, p.
182.

"Who Resteth with the Saints,": King, *Last
Empress*, p. 361.

"as though it were a requiem,": Almedingen,
Empress Alexandra, p. 225.

"Do you know …. to them there.": King, *Last
Empress*, p. 361.

"Nicholas Alexandrovitch, your …. compelled to shoot you.": Deposition of Anatolie Iakimoff in Telberg and Wilton, *Last Days*, p. 187.

"nobility of mind …. all their suffering.": Gilliard, *Thirteen Years*, p. viii.

"They all loved …. the whole family.": Deposition of E.S. Kobylinsky in *Ibid.*, pp. 135-6.

"one of the …. figures in history.": Viroubova, *Memories of the Russian Court*, p. 80.

"He suffered much …. loved him passionately.": Deposition of Sydney Gibbes in Telberg and Wilton, *Last Days of the Romanovs*, p. 56.

"the illness of …. from all eyes.": Gilliard, *Thirteen Years*, p. viii.

"All he suffered …. of other people.": Buxhoeveden, *Life & Tragedy*, p. 150.

"It is one …. and the world." Massie, *Nicholas and Alexandra*, p. 114.

BIBLIOGRAPHY

Alexander, Grand Duke, *Once a Grand Duke*. New York: Cosmopolitan Book Corporation, 1932.

Almedingen, E.M. *The Empress Alexandra 1872-1918: A Study*. London: Hutchinson, 1961.

Benckendorff, Count Paul. *Last Days at Tsarskoe Selo: Being the Personal Notes and Memories of Count Paul Benckendorff, Telling of the Last Sojourn of the Emperor & Empress of Russia at Tsarskoe Selo from March 1 to August 1, 1917*. Translated by Maurice Baring. London: William Heinemann Limited, 1927.

Bing, Edward J., ed., *The Secret Letters of the Last Tsar: Being the Confidential Correspondence Between Nicholas II and His Mother, Dowager Empress Maria Feodorovona*. New York: Longmans, Green, and Co., 1938.

Botkin, Gleb. *The Real Romanovs: As Revealed by the Late Czar's Physician and His Son*. New York: Fleming H. Revell Company, 1931.

Buchanan, Sir George. *My Mission to Russia and Other Diplomatic Memories, Volume I.* London: Cassell and Company, 1923.

--------------------------. *My Mission to Russia and Other Diplomatic Memoirs, Volume II.* London: Cassell and Company, Ltd., 1923.

Buchanan, Meriel. *Recollections of Imperial Russia.* London: Hutchinson & Co., 1923.

Buxhoeveden, Baroness Sophie. *The Life & Tragedy of Alexandra Feodorovna.* London: Longmans, Green and Co., 1929.

Crawford, Rosemary and Donald. *Michael and Natasha: The Life and Love of the Last Tsar of Russia.* Vancouver: Douglas & McIntyre, 1997.

Dehn, Lili, *The Real Tsaritsa.* Boston: Little, Brown, and Company, 1922.

Eagar, M. *Six Years at the Russian Court.* London: Hurst and Blackett, Ltd., 1906.

Gilliard, Pierre. *Thirteen Years at the Russian Court.* New York: George H. Doran & Co., 1921.

King, Greg. *The Last Empress: The Life & Ties of Alexandra Feodorovna, Tsarina of Russia.* New York: Birch Lane Press, 1994.

Kozlov, Vladimir A. and Vladimir M. Khrustalëv, eds., *The Last Diary of Tsaritsa Alexandra*. New Haven, CT: Yale University Press.

Marie, Grand Duchess. *Education of a Princess: A Memoir*. New York: Blue Ribbon Books, Inc., 1933.

Marie, Queen of Roumania, *The Story of My Life*. New York: Charles Scribner's Sons, 1934.

Massie, Robert K. *Nicholas and Alexandra*. New York: Atheneum, 1967.

Maylunas, Andrei and Sergei Mironenko, eds. *A Lifelong Passion: Nicholas and Alexandra, Their Own Story*. London: Weidenfeld & Nicolson, 1996.

Mossolov, A. A. *At the Court of the Last Tsar*. London: Methuen & Co., Ltd., 1935.

Mouchanow, Marfa. *My Empress*. New York: John Lane Company, 1918.

Munsey's Magazine, vol. XXIII, no. 3, June 1905.

Paléologue, Maurice. *An Ambassador's Memoirs, Volume III*. Translated by F.A. Holt. New York: George H. Doran Company, 1923.

Paley, Princess. *Memories of Russia 1916-1919*. London: Herbert Jenkins Ltd., 1924.

Pares, Bernard. *The Fall of the Russian Monarchy: A Study of the Evidence*. London: Jonathan Cape, 1939.

Perry, John Curtis and Constantine Pleshakov, *Flight of the Romanovs: A Family Saga*. New York: Basic Books, 1999.

Pipes, Richard. *The Russian Revolution*. New York: Vintage Books, 1991.

Radziwill, Catherine. *Nicholas II: The Last of the Tsars*. London: Cassell and Company Ltd., 1931.

Rappaport, Helen. *The Romanov Sisters: The Lost Lives of the Daughters of Nicholas and Alexandra*. New York: St. Martin's Press, 2014.

Rodzianko, Mikhail. *The Reign of Rasputin: An Empire's Collapse.* London: A.M. Philpot Ltd., 1927.

Salisbury, Harrison E. *Black Night, White Snow: Russia's Revolutions 1905*-1917, London: Cassell, 1977.

The Sphere, Vol. XX, No. 265, February 18, 1905.

Telberg, George Gustav and Robert Wilton. *The Last Days of the Romanovs*. New York: George H. Doran Company, 1920.

Viroubova, Anna. *Memories of the Russian Court*. London: Macmillan and Co., Ltd., 1923.

Vorres, Ian. *The Last Grand Duchess: Her Imperial Highness Grand Duchess Olga Alexandrovna*. New York: Charles Scriber's Sons, 1964.

Yarmolinsky, Abraham, ed. and translator, *The Memoirs of Count Witte*. Garden City, NY: Doubleday, Page & Company, 1921.

Youssoupoff, Prince Felix. *Lost Splendor*. New York: G.P. Putnam's Sons.

FURTHER READING

Much has been published on Tsar Nicholas II, Tsarina Alexandra, and their family, including first-hand accounts of individuals who knew the family well. Below are some of the books worth looking into for further reading. One of the most famous is Robert K. Massie's classic account from 1967, *Nicholas and Alexandra*, which was adapted into film in 1971, also entitled, 'Nicholas and Alexandra.'

Buxhoeveden, Sophie. *The Life & Tragedy of Alexandra Feodorovna*. London: Longmans, Green and Co., 1929.

Dehn, Lili, *The Real Tsaritsa*. Boston: Little, Brown, and Company, 1922.

Gelardi, Julia P. *Born to Rule: Five Reigning Consorts, Granddaughters of Queen Victoria*. New York: St. Martin's Press, 2005.

------------------. *From Splendor to Revolution: The Romanov Women, 1847-1928*. New York: St. Martin's Press, 2011.

Gilliard, Pierre. *Thirteen Years at the Russian Court*. New York: George H. Doran & Co., 1921.

King, Greg. *The Last Empress: The Life & Times of Alexandra Feodorovna, Tsarina of Russia*. New York: Birch Lane Press, 1994.

Massie, Robert K. *Nicholas and Alexandra*. New York. Atheneum, 1967.

Maylunas, Andrei and Sergei Mironenko. *A Lifelong Passion: Nicholas and Alexandra, Their Own Story*. London: Weidenfeld & Nicolson, 1996.

Mossolov, A.A. *At the Court of the Last Tsar: Being the Memoirs of A.A. Mossolov, Head of the Court Chancellery, 1900-1916*. Edited by A.A. Pilenco. Translated by E.W. Dickes. London: Methuen & Co., Ltd., 1935.

Pipes, Richard. *The Russian Revolution*. New York: Vintage Books, 1991.

Salisbury, Harrison E. *Black Night, White Snow: Russia's Revolutions 1905-1917*, London: Cassell, 1977.

Viroubova, Anna. *Memories of the Russian Court*. London: Macmillan & Company, 1923.

ABOUT THE AUTHOR

Julia P. Gelardi is an independent historian.
After obtaining a Master of Arts degree in history
from Simon Fraser University in Canada, Julia has
written books and articles focusing on European
royalty. She currently resides in Minnesota with her
husband.

BOOKS BY THE AUTHOR

*Born to Rule: Five Reigning Consorts,
Granddaughters of Queen Victoria* (2005)

*In Triumph's Wake: Royal Mothers, Tragic
Daughters, and the Price They Paid for Glory*
(2009)

*From Splendor to Revolution: The Romanov
Women, 1847-1928* (2011)

*Drina & Lilbet; Queen Victoria and Queen
Elizabeth II from Birth to Accession (2018)*

Made in the USA
San Bernardino, CA
06 September 2019